Heartland of a Continent
This first edition belongs to

Name | | Date

ALEXA DORENKAMP PREPARES TO ADVANCE THE COLORS AT A KANSAS RODEO.

Heartland

of a Continent
America's Plains and Prairies

By Ron Fisher

Prepared by the Book Division
National Geographic Society, Washington, D.C.

JOEL SARTORE (BELOW); JOHN EASTCOTT/YVA MOMATIUK (PRECEDING PAGES)

HEARTLAND OF A CONTINENT:
America's Plains and Prairies

By Ron Fisher

Contributing Photographers: Annie Griffiths Belt,
George Olson, Joel Sartore

Published by The National Geographic Society
Gilbert M. Grosvenor,
    President and Chairman of the Board
Michela A. English,
    Senior Vice President
Robert L. Breeden,
    Executive Adviser to the President
    for Publications and Educational Media

Prepared by The Book Division
William R. Gray, *Director*
Margery G. Dunn, *Senior Editor*

Staff for this Special Publication
Toni Eugene, Mary Ann Harrell,
    Managing Editors
Elizabeth L. Newhouse, Barbara A. Payne,
    Gene S. Stuart, *Text Editors*
John G. Agnone, Dennis R. Dimick,
    Illustrations Editors
Cinda Rose, *Art Director*
Victoria Cooper, Ann Nottingham Kelsall,
    Researchers
Richard M. Crum, Tom Melham,
    Cynthia Russ Ramsay, *Picture*
    Legend Writers
Susan I. Friedman, *Map Art and Research*
Joseph F. Ochlak, *Map Research*
Sandra F. Lotterman, *Editorial Assistant*
Karen Dufort Sligh, *Illustrations Assistant*
Lewis R. Bassford,
    Production Project Manager
Heather Guwang, Richard S. Wain,
    Production

Karen F. Edwards, Elizabeth G. Jevons,
    Artemis S. Lampathakis,
    Teresita Cóquia Sison,
    Marilyn J. Williams, *Staff Assistants*

Diane Coleman, *Indexer*

Manufacturing and Quality Management
George V. White, *Director;* John T. Dunn,
    Associate Director; Vincent P. Ryan,
    Manager; and R. Gary Colbert

*HIGH SCHOOL GRIDIRON STAR TODD
HIMMELBERG SAVORS A WIN IN NEBRASKA.*

*PRECEDING PAGES: LIGHTNING ILLUMINATES
A SUNSET SKY IN MANITOBA, CANADA.*

Edmonton

ALBERTA

SASKATCHEWAN

MANITOBA

Saskatoon

Swift
Current

Regina

Winnipeg

ROCKY

*N*orth America's plains and prairies
rolled west to the Rocky Mountains in
waves of grasses until settlers plowed and
homesteaded the heartland; only patches
of original grassland survive. Variations
in rainfall and elevation determine the type
of vegetation. Today, the immense sweep of
country produces food for much of the world.

Fort
Benton

Helena

Great Falls

MONTANA

Fort Union
Trading Post

NORTH
DAKOTA

Bismarck

Fargo Moorhead

St. Paul

WISCONSIN

MOUNTAINS

Custer Battlefield
Nat. Mon.

SOUTH
DAKOTA

Columbia

Minneapolis

MINNESOTA

MICHIGAN

Mississippi R.

Wright

Pierre

Volga

Mason City

Madison

Lansing

WYOMING

Mt. Rushmore
Nat. Mem.

Missouri R.

Sioux City

IOWA

Chicago

Laramie Cheyenne

North Platte R.

NEBRASKA

Grand
Island

Des
Moines

ILLINOIS

Crown
Point

Milford

South Platte R.

ROCKY

Denver

Lincoln

Kansas City

MISSOURI

Springfield

Indianapolis

INDIANA

COLORADO

Colorado
Springs

Salina

Topeka

Kansas
City

Jefferson
City

MOUNTAINS

KANSAS

Lawrence

Santa Fe

OKLAHOMA

Tulsa

ARKANSAS

Mississippi R.

NEW MEXICO

Oklahoma
City

Little
Rock

Lubbock

Denton

Post

Abilene

Dallas

Winters

TEXAS

Austin

U.S.

CANADA

UNITED
STATES

MEXICO

Shortgrass and Mixed-grass Prairie

Tallgrass Prairie

Prairie–Forest Transition

0   500 km

0   300 mi

Contents

Yesterday

Land of Hope and Sorrow

They paid a price for their new land.

It was a year and a half, in 1850, before Abigail Malick could bring herself to write to family members back in Illinois, telling of the trip across the Great Plains to Oregon and of the fate of her son Hiram, 17. "Hiram drounded in the Plat River At the Mouth of Dear Krick. He went A-swimming with some other boys of the Compeny that we Trailed with And he swum Acrost the river and the Water run very fast And he could not reach this side. . . . And one young Man took A pole And started to him And the water ran so fast that he thought he Could not swim eney more so he returned And left him to his fate. And the other boys Called to him and said O hiram O swim. And he said o my god I cannot eney More. They said that he went down in the water seven or eight times before he drounded. And then he said o my god O lord gesus receive My Soul for I am no More." She added, "It has Almost kild Me. . . ."

They paid a heavy price. I stood on a sunny hillside in northern Montana with crickets chirping at my feet and cattails nodding in the breeze alongside a muddy slough. I found the very spot where Chief Joseph of the Nez Perce is said to have stood to address the remnants of his band: "It is cold and we have no blankets. The little children are freezing to death. . . . Hear me, my chiefs! I am tired. My heart is sick and sad. From where the sun now stands, I will fight no more forever."

Pioneers and Indians. And cowboys. E. C. "Teddy Blue" Abbott, an old Montana cowboy, remembered what it was like. "I heard a story once about a school teacher who asked one of these old Texas cow dogs to tell her all about how he punched cows on the trail. She said: 'Oh Mister So-and-So, didn't the boys used to have a lot of fun riding their ponies?' He said: 'Madam, there wasn't any boys or ponies. They was all horses and men.' "

Horses, men, cowboys, Indians, and pioneers—the cast of characters could hardly be more familiar to us. Their stories became the myths of

Remnant of a once vast landscape, Indian grass sways against a sunset sky at Audubon Prairie, a 600-acre preserve in Minnesota. By 1900 the steel plow had broken the prairie sod, and fields of native tallgrasses gave way to farmland.

PRECEDING PAGES: On a cattle drive in the dry, shortgrass prairie of the Great Plains, Montana ranchers move a herd of cows and calves to winter pasture.

moviemakers and novelists, and the stage on which they acted—the continent's heartland—is almost the landscape of cliché. The corn as high as an elephant's eye, the amber waves of grain, the Dakota blizzard and Montana's Big Sky, the rivers, the prairies, the plains, the cattleman's son and the farmer's daughter—we've seen them all.

The heartland—the flat central slab of North America, what writer John McPhee calls "the continent's enduring core"—stretches from the Panhandle of Texas up into Canada and from the Rocky Mountains in the west to the northwest corner of Indiana in the east. It includes parts of 16 states and 3 Canadian provinces. When Columbus arrived, a third of what would become the 48 United States was grassland—perhaps a million square miles.

Half is plains and half prairies. It's been pointed out that the eastern half of America offers no suggestion of the western half, so dissimilar are the two. Travelers moving westward noted the gradual change in the grasses; as the countryside became drier, the grass grew shorter. The distinguished historian Walter Prescott Webb wrote, "For the most part the boundary between the timber and the prairie lies between the ninety-fourth and ninety-eighth meridians." The first to record the change may have been Lewis and Clark. Starting out, they referred to any open country as "prairie," but to these Easterners prairie meant an area bounded by forest. When they came at last to the awesome stretches of treeless country farther west, "prairie" didn't seem adequate, and they began referring to the "great plains."

Some semantic confusion remains. The grasslands that cover the Great Plains are often referred to as prairies. So, while there are extensive prairies in the Great Plains, there are no Great Plains in the prairies.

Look in any U.S. atlas today at North and South Dakota or at Nebraska and Kansas, and you can see—at about the 100th meridian—the change. Counties are bigger to the west, roads straighter, towns fewer. East of the 100th meridian you'll hear meadowlarks; to the west you'll see magpies.

Historically, in the east grew tallgrass prairies, dominated by big bluestem; in the west were shortgrass plains, grazed by bison; and where they overlapped mixed grasses grew, dominated by little bluestem. "The species have changed," wrote naturalist John Madsen, "but the essential prairie forms have not. Iowa's prairie country still produces tallgrasses in the form of corn; central Kansas grows mid-height grasses in the form of wheat; and the Great Plains is still a major producer of bovids." Now they're cattle instead of bison.

You come close to finding the line between the plains and the prairies by looking at men's hats: Farmers wear baseball caps with, often, the names of farm machinery manufacturers on them, and ranchers wear cowboy hats. In Winters, Texas—which is within five miles of the 100th meridian—I stopped at a Dairy Queen that had four pickups parked in front. Inside were four men. Two were wearing baseball caps and two, cowboy hats. Eureka!

The line between the prairies and the plains is also a function of elevation. The 25-inch-per-year rainfall line occurs roughly at about 1,500 feet above sea level—that is about halfway across Nebraska, Kansas, and Oklahoma. Continue westward, and you climb about ten feet a mile until you reach the Rocky Mountains. In Colorado, I drove west on U.S. 50, climbing higher and higher through little towns: Granada 3,483 feet; La Junta 4,066; Rocky Ford 4,178; Manzanola 4,252. From Pueblo to Colorado Springs, the solid wall of the Rockies was on my left. I rode the train there up to Pikes Peak—and the Great Plains spread out before me like a billiard table.

I was exploring the heartland. Usually, my routine was to fly to a large city, rent a car, and devote a couple of weeks to making a big circle. The cruise control I found to be a handy invention in the Great Plains, where highways stretch before you as straight as an Indian's arrow for miles and miles. I listened to the accents of heartlanders. In a bar in Texas, a cowboy beside me ordered a beer: "Curs Lot, please."

I became acquainted with the music of the heartland—*If you're gonna do me wrong, do it right!*—and the food, which is cheap, plentiful, and delicious, though it's difficult to find a good cup of coffee. Every small town has a café that, for five or six dollars, will set before you a heaped and steaming meal of pork chop, mashed potatoes, green beans, coleslaw, iced tea, coffee, and pie. My travels became a quest for the perfect piece of chocolate cream pie.

Heartlanders have long been known for their friendliness, and I had it confirmed; in seven months, I encountered no rudeness at all.

By chance, 1990 turned out to be the all-time record year of the tornado; 1,126 were logged. In Oklahoma, many an evening, a state map would appear on the TV screen, with the counties under alert colored in; I could watch the tornado warnings march across the state toward me.

Ages ago, dinosaurs roamed broad grasslands here in the heartland. Eventually, mammals replaced them. At Agate Fossil Beds National Monument in western Nebraska, the brochure reads, "Nineteen million years ago strange creatures walked a Miocene savanna. . . ." I trudged upward on a path lined with evening primrose and prairie groundsel to a dig supervised by paleontologist Robert Hunt of Lincoln. Grids covered a small area on the flank of a hill overlooking the Niobrara River, here barely five feet wide. Dr. Hunt and his colleagues were uncovering the dens of *Daphoenodon*, extinct bear dogs. "Bear dogs had skeletons similar to today's bears, but with some features more like wolves'," Dr. Hunt said.

Not far from there, in eastern Montana, scientists had recently uncovered the world's most complete skeleton of *Tyrannosaurus rex*. And in Dinosaur Provincial Park in Alberta I saw a fossilized hadrosaur in a bed of rock, its duck-billed head missing. Near the park, I bought a sausage roll and chips at the Dinosaur Country Store and ate at a picnic table. A sleek blue-black magpie came to an adjacent table, laid its head on the table as if it were going to take a nap, and sipped from a tiny puddle. *(Continued on page 20)*

Mist mellows a quiet
moment as a young bareback
rider slacks up on the reins to
let her pony drink from the
Jacks Fork River, near
Eminence, Missouri. Horses
and mules were the mainstay
of family farms for decades,
pulling implements such as
plows and mowers. Replaced
by tractors as family fortunes
permitted, the animals
nearly disappeared from the
midwestern landscape by the
end of World War II. But in
rural America today, horses
have made a comeback as
recreational animals.

*B*ig bluestem glistens with morning dew (opposite) at Cedar Sand Prairie in Colorado. A predominant plant of the tallgrass prairie, six-foot-tall bluestem provides nutritious forage for cattle. Purple coneflowers (above) bloom in a preserve owned by the Minnesota Nature Conservancy. Plumes of seeds sprout from the spent flowers of purple avens, commonly known as prairie smoke (below). Once degraded by overgrazing, these native wildflowers and grasses now flourish in prairie preserves on the northern plains.

FOLLOWING PAGES: Camouflaged by color and shape, a walkingstick hangs from the head of a prairie grass above a coneflower. The insect, a master of disguise, instinctively chooses a setting that makes it inconspicuous to its enemies.

ANNIE GRIFFITHS BELT (TOP); JIM BRANDENBURG (ABOVE); THOMAS R. ROSBURG (OPPOSITE)

Magpies are said to remember for a week where they've stashed a morsel of food. Zebulon Pike accused them of pecking holes in his mules.

Glaciers shaped the heartland, too. I spent an afternoon in northern Iowa with Doug Harr, wildlife biologist with the state's Department of Natural Resources, tracing part of Iowa's Glacial Landmarks Trail. Glaciers last covered this area for about 1,500 years between 14,000 and 12,500 years ago. At the Freda Haffner Kettlehole State Preserve, we walked across a grassy hilltop pasture to a huge, bowl-shaped depression. "This is probably the best example of a kettle out in the open prairie anywhere in the Midwest," said Doug. "The ice cap was probably about 5,000 feet thick here. It tapered down to a thickness of about 600 feet at its foot, which was located about where the state capitol is."

"You mean Des Moines?"

"No. Those hills there by the river *in* Des Moines that the capitol complex sits on. That was the terminus of the Des Moines lobe of the Wisconsin glacier. Here at Kettlehole, when the glacier retreated, it left a huge pocket of ice that sat in place and slowly melted." In the valley below us, the Little

Sioux River traced a tree-lined course. Later in our drive through the rolling cornfields and sloughs of Iowa, Doug said, "Here we're in the southern terminus of prairie pothole country, which extends up into central Canada. Places where little chunks of ice sat. It's been so recently that the glaciers left, that in this area the natural drainage patterns haven't had time to form. Given another hundred thousand years, even without farming, natural erosion would drain these things.

"Once there were about two and a half million acres of wetlands in Iowa alone, but most were drained back around the turn of the century. We're down to maybe 35 or 40 thousand acres now, a loss of nearly 99 percent."

The dinosaurs and the glaciers are long gone, but the prairies and the plains endure, with their rich soils and hardy grasses. A square yard of prairie soil just four inches deep may contain roots enough to stretch 20 miles if placed end to end. Grass survives grazers because its leaves grow from the base; if the tips are eaten, growth continues from below. Cordgrass grew so tall in the prairie a horse could disappear in it. A square mile of mixed prairie in eastern Colorado yielded 143 species of forbs—non-grass herbs.

Here the buffalo roamed. There may once have been 60 million bison in the heartland, but the herds that were said to reach to the horizon were made up of smaller groups of 50 to 200 animals. There was always open space among them. Bulls stood six feet at the shoulder and weighed about a ton. Cortéz may have been the first European to see bison—in 1519 in the menagerie of Moctezuma in the Valley of Mexico.

Pronghorns were here, and prairie dogs in their uncountable millions. Prairie chickens boomed on display stages, and cranes and geese filled the skies with beauty and song. Prairie birds such as meadowlarks and bobolinks commonly sing on the wing, for there are few places to perch; most forest birds sing from perches. And today, each prairie state boasts at least 100 species of grasshoppers; Kansas may have about 300.

"This whole country, back when the Indians were here, was just like this," said George Woodfin. "That'd a been something to see." We were standing at the edge of a Texas highway looking out over George's 2,500-acre field of virgin prairie. "It's never been plowed. It was my uncle, really, that saved it. He liked it so much he just baled hay off it every year. Made enough to pay the taxes on it." It was the day before Easter, and the grasses were about six inches tall. "This'll be five feet tall by July, when we cut and bale it," said George. "In winter, 3,000 Canada geese stay out there all winter long. There are small pools, just enough for them to drink."

Excavating fossils in Nebraska, a team from the state museum brushes ten-million-year-old volcanic ash from rhinoceros bones at the site of an ancient water hole. At the time of that eruption, a savanna stretched across the Great Plains.

I went for a walk across George's prairie, scaring up meadowlarks, which lob their songs toward intruders like gifts. It was hot and silent, though somewhere a farmer was hammering something metal. In *Little House on the Prairie*, Laura Ingalls Wilder wrote, "Day after day they traveled in Kansas, and saw nothing but the rippling grass and the enormous sky. In a perfect circle the sky curved down to the level land, and the wagon was in the circle's exact middle."

To the west of the prairies, until the middle of the 19th century, was what early mapmakers called desert. Washington Irving thought it bleak: "This region, which resembles one of the ancient steppes of Asia, has not inaptly been termed The Great American Desert. It spreads forth into undulating and treeless plains and desolate sandy wastes, wearisome to the eye from their extent and monotony." Settlers had never seen anything like it, and the tools and mental outlooks they brought with them needed revising.

They found on the plains and prairies kinship-based societies of American Indians. Most followed the bison on their seasonal movement, using the animals for practically everything they needed—food, clothing, utensils, receptacles. Their languages were so numerous that no one knew them all, and they had developed a system of sign language that, according to historian James Mooney, "for all ordinary purposes, hardly fell short of the perfection of a spoken language."

Since they had no written language, the imbalance between what was recorded of their thoughts and experiences and those of Europeans is great. Whites wrote everything down; Indians wrote nothing. Artist George Catlin thought that the Indian's "mind is a beautiful blank on which anything can be written." There's no record of what the Indians thought of Catlin.

Largely peaceable for centuries, things had changed by early in the 18th century. Says Webb: "Then came the horse; and overnight, so to speak, the whole life and economy of the Plains Indians was changed. Steam and electricity have not wrought a greater revolution in the ways of civilized life than the horse did in the savage life of the Plains." Tribes became more warlike with their new mobility, and animosities and alliances were in flux when explorers and settlers began arriving.

American Indians left their mark all over. Thousands of burial mounds dot the prairie, mostly along the rivers. And Indian words add color to the landscape. David Costello, a Nebraskan, writes: "For many years I lived in Nemaha County. Frequently I visited the place where my father was born in Otoe County. Regularly I traveled to Nehawka, Weeping Water,

Nestled in the grasses of South Dakota's Custer State Park, a lone skull evokes the slaughter of the millions of bison that once roamed the plains. A herd of 1,400— one of the largest publicly owned in the United States—grazes the park today.

Tecumseh, or Omaha without realizing that these were Indian names."

They left artistic evidence, too. Near Jeffers, Minnesota, I strolled through a group of nearly 2,000 petroglyphs, pecked into slabs of exposed quartzite. Some are very old, dating back perhaps to 3000 B.C.; others were made between A.D. 900 and 1750. There are hundreds of stick figures, many armed with an atlatl, a spear-throwing tool. Birds and other animals, perhaps a horse—much looks like doodling, and it must have been pleasant to sit in the breeze with a view of what would one day be called the Little Cottonwood River, with the sun warm on your back, idly pecking.

Traders, establishing posts and forts, were among the first white settlers in Indian country. Fort Union, established in 1829, was fortunate in its location, a quiet site of hills at the confluence of the Yellowstone and Missouri Rivers in what is today North Dakota. At the fort, now kept up by the National Park Service, I climbed to the parapet in solitude and imagined the prairie covered with the tepees and smoky fires of Indians and trappers.

Fort Union seems to have been visited by most of the notable travelers of the 19th century. John James Audubon stopped by, as did Prince Maximilian of Wied, who noticed "the handsome American flag." Catlin wrote: "a very substantial Fort. . . . the continued roar of cannon for half an hour, and the shrill yells of the half-affrighted savages who lined the shores, presented a scene of the most thrilling appearance." It was a cosmopolitan place. Rudolph Kurz, a Swiss painter employed as a clerk by the American Fur Company, said: "It is quite a while before one knows all the various terms for fresh meat, cured meat, lard, corn, water, 'open the door,' etc., in seven different languages."

The U.S. Army had forts of its own throughout the West. During the Indian wars, the troopers were volunteers. Between 1865 and the 1890s many were recent immigrants, and some were felons. A sergeant remembered: "Some were good and some were bad, and some were very bad."

There was no mystery about the roots of the Indian wars that bloodied the heartland. Maj. Gen. Philip H. Sheridan, who served many years as a commander in the West, wrote: "We took away their country and their means of support, broke up their mode of living, their habits of life, introduced disease and decay among them, and it was for this and against this that they made war."

The troopers respected their Indian foes as warriors and mingled with them between engagements, enough to find them fascinating and even admirable. But goldfields and fertile lands drew ever more whites into Indian

territory, and bloody warfare was inevitable. The Indian wars were well reported by correspondents who had developed their specialty during the Civil War. Henry Stanley, who would later greet Dr. Livingstone famously in Africa, covered the fighting on the Kansas plains for the *Missouri Democrat*. He wrote of Lt. Col. George Armstrong Custer (major general by honorary rank), "A certain impetuosity and undoubted courage are his principal characteristics." Another correspondent, John F. Finerty, wrote that the journalists had to share the life of the soldiers, that they had to be "ready to fight Sitting Bull or Satan when the trouble begins, for God and the United States hate non-combatants."

It came to a head in Montana. Custer came spoiling for a fight—and found it. On June 25, 1876, he and about 220 of his regiment retreated to a grassy hill overlooking the Little Bighorn River. Hundreds of Sioux and Cheyenne warriors of Sitting Bull and Crazy Horse surrounded them. It was one of the last armed efforts of the Indians to repel the whites from their lands. More than 260 soldiers and attached personnel died in the course of the battle, including Custer and every member of his immediate command.

Mid-century witnessed migrations of Easterners crossing the prairies and plains on their way to the promised lands in the West. Though the decades of expansion brought tragedy to the Indians, we still hold a romantic notion of the pioneers. In a book of recollections, Herbert Quick wrote: "They turned their faces to the west which they had for generations seen at sunset through traceries of the twigs and leafage of the primal forests, and finally stepped out into the open. . . ." *(Continued on page 30)*

*B*ison graze the shortgrasses of a Wyoming range. In a friendly greeting, prairie dogs (left) nuzzle each other. A pronghorn (right) nibbles a shrub in South Dakota. Once numbering in the millions, these prairie species thrive today in protected preserves.

FOLLOWING PAGES: State Highway 56 traces the Santa Fe Trail across wide-open Kansas.

NGS PHOTOGRAPHER JAMES P. BLAIR (ABOVE); ANNIE GRIFFITHS BELT (LEFT); JIM BRANDENBURG (OPPOSITE); GEORGE OLSON (FOLLOWING PAGES)

By 1869, when the transcontinental railroad was completed, some 350,000 people had journeyed westward on overland trails. The Santa Fe and Oregon Trails felt their tread, as they faced hardship to spread the American empire westward. Some were less than worthy. Within a hundred miles of the Missouri River, a forty-niner wrote, most of his fellows had become "cross, peevish, sullen, boisterous, giddy, profane, dirty, vulgar, ragged, mustachioed, be-whiskered, idle, petulant, quarrelsome, unfaithful, disobedient, refractory, careless, contrary, stubborn, hungry, and without the fear of God. . . ."

Common injuries claimed children, who fell beneath the wheels of moving wagons. Others died of measles, scarlet fever, smallpox, typhus, or cholera. *O bury me not on the lone prairie,* says the old song, *Where the wild coyotes will howl o'er me. . . .*

Guidebooks were published to help the pioneers on their way. In one, readers learned that, while fording rivers, "the condition of the quicksand may be ascertained by sending an intelligent man over the fording-place. . . . A man incurs no danger in walking over quicksand provided he step rapidly." One trembles for the unintelligent and the credulous. "Mules are good swimmers," pioneers read, "unless they happen, by plunging off a high bank, to get water in their ears, when they are often drowned."

In northern Wyoming, I stood on a grassy hilltop and got a look at what the pioneers' wagons must have looked like. As part of its centennial celebration, Wyoming had put together a train of 93 vehicles—carts, covered wagons, buggies, and a small stagecoach—to traverse a part of the state. I caught up with them at Fort Phil Kearny. More than 500 people from 27 states, as well as Canada and Australia, were participating. They had unhitched their wagons and pitched their tents in a small valley with the Bighorn Mountains rising beyond and huge white clouds floating overhead. The white canvas of their tents matched the white canvas of their wagons. Horses whinnied back and forth from either end of the encampment. Participants were in costume: women in gingham dresses and sunbonnets, men in jeans and suspenders. They all looked very authentic, though I did see a cavalryman—tight blue trousers, boots, stripes on his sleeve—emerge from a portable toilet. Schoolchildren brought for a field trip made their way through the encampment in single file, herded by teachers with whistles.

Homes on the range: Plains Indians, like the Sioux portrayed beside their tepees (opposite), followed the bison herds, setting up camp in the portable dwellings. In an 1886 photograph, homesteaders pose outside their sod house at Woods Park, Nebraska. Cheap land lured settlers west and into conflict with the Indians.

After the Homestead Act of 1862, settlers flocked to the West. In 1910 the federal land office in Great Falls, Montana, processed a thousand claims a month. But drive today along U.S. 2 in northern Montana, and you see the homesteaders' sagging barns and houses, abandoned and crumbling. As farming pushed west into the plains, wrote Patricia Nelson Limerick in *The Legacy of Conquest*, "thousands were deceived into thinking that securing a piece of land was all that was necessary to make a competence for the owner." The requirement that settlers live on their 160-acre quarter sections ensured that families would be widely scattered on the already lonely prairies. The sod houses were by definition dirty, and dust covered everything.

The climate could be brutal. Though most of the heartland is temperate, extremes occur. Temperatures in North Dakota have ranged from minus 60°F to 120°F—a difference of 180 degrees. Blizzards, a heartland phenomenon, are largely a product of the prairie wind, which can continue at gale force long after the snow has stopped. Drifts 15 feet deep are not unusual.

Times were almost always bad, it seemed. Perhaps hardest was what Isabella Bird, a celebrated traveler from England, called "the extinction of childhood." A Kansas farmer bragged about his son: "Little Baz can run all over, fetch up cows out of the stock fields, or oxen, carry in stove wood and climb in the corn crib and feed the hogs and go on errands down to his grand ma's." At the time Little Baz was two years, three months old. As an adult, a woman remembered a terrible night in her childhood while her father was away. "Mother awakened me in the night and had to have assistance. She gave birth to a baby—stillborn. She had to get a little box that we had, and we placed the baby in it, and in the morning before the other children were awake, she sent me out to bury it not far from the house. I was about twelve years old at the time."

Stephen Vincent Benét wrote, "This was frontier, and this / And this, your house, was frontier."

They paid a price. Walter Prescott Webb sympathized with the women: "The life of the farm woman was intolerable, unutterably lonely. . . . The wind, the sand, the drought, the unmitigated sun, and the boundless expanse of a horizon . . . seemed to overwhelm the women with a sense of desolation, insecurity, and futility."

"This," said a newcomer, "would be a fine country if we just had water." And the disillusioned resident growled, "So would hell." The drought that hit the Great Plains in the 1930s was the worst ever recorded there and lasted seven years in some places. The plains became for a few years the Dust Bowl. "Black blizzards" rolled across the heartland, and dust settled on ships 300 miles out in the Atlantic. Only the cowboys appeared to have fun. John Moses, who grew up to be a respected Texas rancher, said: "I thought the biggest life in the world would be to live like a freighter or cowpuncher. I wanted to cuss and chew tobacco and sleep out in the mud." And Teddy Blue Abbott remembered: "I went in and cut a big swathe in town, most of the time with one girl. I do not mean that she was a decent girl; we knew very few of those. . . . I had plenty of good horses to ride, and the girls said I was the best-looking cowboy on the Powder River. And they cleaned me down to my spurs." The reality of their world does not always square with our image of the clean-cut, devout pioneer.

A contemporary saying ran: "There is no Sunday west of St. Louis—no God west of Fort Smith." In the state capitol building in Pierre I admired a large mural depicting the first Christian prayer in South Dakota: In a river-boat, buckskinned mourners cluster around a fallen comrade while a haloed Jesus, in the bow of the boat, peers sadly down on them.

They paid a price. The Sergeant Floyd Monument on the Missouri River near Sioux City, Iowa, is dedicated to the only member of the Lewis and Clark Expedition to lose his life. I read the inscription, "Graves of such men are pilgrim shrines, shrines to no class or creed confined." There was a broad view of the river below, and grain elevators on the opposite shore.

In a lonely spot near the confluence of the Yellowstone and Powder Rivers in Montana, where Captain Clark camped on the night of July 30, 1806, I found a tiny cemetery preserving the remains of several buffalo hunters. "On 9-5-21 GR McDonald marked these nameless graves with dated head-stones. One killed by Indians in 1878; two killed in a quarrel at the Folley roadhouse in 1880; three died natural deaths at roadhouse in 1881."

Of the players on the heartland stage, the American Indians are hardest to know—they are viewed with such a load of romance and guilt. And of the Indians, Crazy Horse is probably the most enigmatic. Mystical and single-minded, he resisted the white advance to the last. It was said that a wild coyote followed him like a dog, and bullets and arrows vanished before they reached him. He never compromised, and died, still resisting, at Fort Robinson in Nebraska. He never allowed himself to be photographed. He said, "We preferred our own way of living." No one knows where he is buried.

Not far from Mount Rushmore in the Black Hills of South Dakota, the family of sculptor Korczak Ziolkowski is completing a gigantic equestrian statue of Crazy Horse that Korczak had begun carving from a mountain more than three decades before his death in 1982. I stopped by in late October to see how they were coming along, and found much still to be done. An early snowstorm was moving into the Black Hills, and the shaggy backs of a small herd of bison alongside the road were getting a coat of white frosting. Because of the weather I rushed my visit. From below I could see the base of the mountain, and I could see an outline of the muzzle of the stallion. But Crazy Horse, elusive as always, was invisible in the softly falling snow.

FOLLOWING PAGES: In a tradition as American as apple pie, the Gaul family gathers for Fourth of July festivities in Independence, Iowa. Each year, the Gauls welcome friends and neighbors to their front porch to watch the parade.

The Prairies

Bounty of the Grassland

Six percent of Iowans think it's the heat; eighty-seven percent say it's the humidity. This according to the Iowa Poll, conducted periodically since 1943 by the *Des Moines Register*. In 1980, asked which from a list of notables they would like to have as a weekend guest, Iowans' three top choices were then Governor Robert Ray, former Governor Harold Hughes, and Ann Landers. Sixty-five percent of Iowans have prayed for rain. Seventy percent swear when they hurt themselves or become angry. Eighty-nine percent, touchingly, would marry the same person. Only five percent say they were personally affected by the death of Sid Vicious, but fifty percent felt the loss of Elvis. Sixty-four percent, given the choice, would choose to be reincarnated as themselves.

A capital city of nearly 200,000 people, home to Drake University, more than 60 insurance companies, and an art center designed by Eliel Saarinen (with wings by I. M. Pei and Richard Meier), Des Moines is joining the trend of cities in the northern prairies in building enclosed skywalks between its downtown buildings. The city even holds a yearly golf tournament in the maze of walkways. Off one of them, I found the *Register* offices and Ann Selzer, who conducts the poll for the newspaper. She let me rummage through her files. At least four times a year she and her staff call a new batch of 800 carefully selected Iowans and conduct a 15-minute interview, from which they hope to get 12 to 15 stories.

"We make it a point not to call on Friday nights; there's usually nobody home except elderly women, and we get a skewed sample," said Ann. Most of the questions are of a serious nature, having to do with national or state issues or politics, but many delve for lighter fare. "It's especially fun when we can play our findings off against national data," she added. "For example, eleven percent of Iowans name their cars, which is exactly the same percentage as Californians."

Bold in bronze, "the Sower," atop the state capitol in Lincoln, Nebraska, symbolizes farming, the essence of a homesteader's life on the prairie.

PRECEDING PAGES: Pheasant hunters John Sartore and Mark Mankin turn homeward at sunset beneath roiling autumn clouds. Nebraskans relish pheasant season. The sharp air invigorates; the sudden flurry of a flushed bird taking wing in a frosty field makes hearts pound. Introduced into the area in the early 1900s, the hardy, adaptable birds thrive in the grain-rich farmland and prairie habitat.

"Our mission is to inform readers about what it's like to be an Iowan, to be a mirror of their daily lives," she said. "We want to get to the soft underbelly of the Iowa psyche."

Historian Dorothy Schwieder has written, "If the Middle West is the nation's heartland, then perhaps Iowa is the heart itself, pulsating quietly, slowly, and evenly, blending together the physical and social features of the entire region."

Iowa is in the heart of the heartland breadbasket, where the world's most successful agriculture is practiced. The breadbasket produces one-third of the world's soybeans, three-fourths of the continent's wheat and corn, and many of its cattle and pigs. The land is amazingly fertile. One acre in central Illinois can produce twice as much corn as an acre in central Virginia. The topsoil here may be seven feet deep, and some of the grasses grow roots half an inch thick. The farming economy in the breadbasket is routinely tied to events on the other side of the world, such as severe weather in Siberia. There are 2,140,420 farms in the U.S. now, but they have grown in size from an average of 168 acres in 1940 to 461 acres in 1990. Less than 3 percent of the American population could be called farmers.

Many of them live in Iowa, and it's the soft underbelly of their psyche that the *Register* is after. It was in Iowa that I found the Boondocks Motel, and it was apparently in Iowa that the word "blizzard" acquired its modern meaning. In 1829 a blizzard meant a heavy blow; in the Civil War, a volley of musketry. O. C. Bates, editor of the Estherville *Northern Vindicator,* applied it to a storm of wind and snow after the town was cut off by drifts on March 14, 1870. It was in Iowa that I found the house that appears in Grant Wood's famous painting "American Gothic"—ironically, occupied by a representative of Mary Kay Cosmetics. As you cross the Mississippi into Iowa at Keokuk you see a sign that reads: "Iowa—Come Explore the Heartland."

It was in Iowa that I was born, raised, and educated. I learned that, while there are a Harpers Ferry, a Pikes Peak, a Cornell, and a Monticello in Iowa, they exist elsewhere, too.

You can reach Iowa by ferry. I rode one summer day across the roiling Mississippi from Cassville, Wisconsin, on a small car ferry. Brian Harris, in shorts, T-shirt, cap, and apron with pockets for change, collected the toll. He teaches eighth grade during the school year, in the same school he attended. "Our attendance is about half what it was when I went there," he told me.

I drove north along the river that quiet Sunday morning. *I put a golden band on the right left hand this time,* sang the radio. The river was high for the season, and branches on island trees touched the water, like the hems of skirts. Cabins atop pilings lined the bank. In public areas, benches for fishermen faced the river.

The *Des Moines Register* is deeply involved in another Iowa institution: RAGBRAI, the *Register's* Annual Great Bicycle Ride Across Iowa. Like Superbowls, they're numbered with Roman numerals, and 1990's was XVIII. Cyclists take a week in summer to ride across Iowa, each year by a different route. Towns along the way vie with one another to provide them with watermelon, ice water, and shady campsites. In 1990 the number of riders was limited to 7,500—which is still a lot on narrow Iowa roads. Outside West Bend I paused to watch them go by. The country was perfectly flat in all directions and the highway straight and black. There was never a time that I couldn't see a couple of hundred riders. I noticed a lot of pink shoulders, more elderly people than I expected, and a number of hunks and hunkettes in pink-and-black spandex. Only the hum of their tires and their murmured conversations broke the stillness. Several pulled bike trailers filled with their supplies or toddlers.

Iowa, by the way, has many of the nation's finest examples of buildings designed by architects of the Prairie School. During the first 20 years or so of the 20th century, a number of midwestern architects—led by Frank Lloyd Wright—developed a style of building meant to reflect what Wright called the "natural beauty" of the prairie. They emphasized the relationship between building and landscape, working to incorporate structures into their sites. "These designs," writes H. Allen Brooks, past president of the Society of Architectural Historians, "are characterized by long, unbroken wall surfaces, continuous bands of leaded casement windows, and low, spreading roofs which, Wright explained, would provide protection from extremes of weather and 'give a sense of shelter in the look of a building.' He extended the lines of the house into the landscape itself with terraces, pergolas, and covered porches, so that it 'began to associate with the ground and became natural to its prairie site.' "

I visited a number of these buildings. In Oak Park, Illinois, a suburb of Chicago, I walked through a neighborhood thick with Prairie School houses, including Wright's own home and studio. On broad farmlands near Spring Green, Wisconsin, I toured Taliesin, Wright's principal home after 1911 and site of the architectural school he established in 1932. And on a limestone bluff overlooking a bend in the Wapsipinicon River in eastern Iowa, I visited Cedar Rock, a home built by Wright between 1948 and 1950. It is one of the most complete designs Wright ever did: He designed not only the house, but also the furniture, selected the draperies and carpets, and even chose accessories.

Finally, in Mason City, Iowa, hometown of composer Meredith Willson, I found the Rock Crest/Rock Glen subdivision, an 18-acre development straddling Willow Creek near the heart of the city. One side of the creek is a bluff, Rock Crest, and the other a gently sloping bank, Rock Glen. A number of Prairie School architects—including Wright himself, Walter Burley Griffin, and Barry Byrne—had a hand in the design and construction of the houses hereabouts.

*C*oncern over stunted corn prompts a meeting on the Dickkut farm in Marshall County, Iowa. Timely rainfall and fertile prairie soil, which nourished native tallgrass long ago, help make Iowa one of the nation's most productive farm states. Many farmers use herbicides to control weeds, but carryover from previous years can harm crops. In one of the Dickkuts' fields, the past season's weed poison, applied to a soybean crop, stunted corn roots. John Creswell, an Iowa State University extension crop specialist (left), examines the damage with Herb Dickkut, Sr. (in plaid shirt), his son Herb, and the Marshalltown Co-op sales representative, Paul Gaunt (in light jacket).

It was a bright sunny Sunday morning when I visited Mason City. At nearby Clear Lake I paused to watch a church group depart on *Lady of the Lake*, a paddle wheeler. Far away across the lake a fleet of identical sailboats were racing; they looked like a flock of white birds skimming low across the water. In a restaurant, I heard a woman say to her husband, "She doesn't even have her palm leaves unpacked yet, and next Sunday's Palm Sunday!"

The James Blythe house in Rock Crest/Rock Glen was designed and built by Griffin in 1913–14 and called by Brooks "a significant monument in the annals of American architecture." It belongs now to a doctor, Robert McCoy, and his wife, Bonnie, and I imposed on them for a tour. We sat first in the living room, looking out upon the green and forested glen of Willow Creek. "To me, the Prairie School was a conscious attempt to create an American architecture," said Dr. McCoy. "There's nothing here that's Gothic, no Greek Revival, no pseudo-Tudor; this was American from scratch." We strolled through the house and grounds as Dr. McCoy pointed out features. "I don't know if you noticed," he said, "but there's no large foyer. You came in the back door, and from there you could have gone into the basement, the garage, the kitchen, the living room, or out the front door without passing through another room.

"Note all the open space," he said. "The kitchen is the only room—other than the bedrooms and baths—that has four walls. That was to

separate the family from the maid—something everybody had in those days." I asked about maintenance of the house, which is built of reinforced concrete. "No problem. Our roof doesn't even leak, which is supposed to be a hallmark of Prairie School houses."

Of heartland architecture, the most poignant structures are the huge wooden barns. Each year sees fewer and fewer, for, like dinosaurs unable to adapt, they no longer fill the needs of farmers. When every farm had a few head of cattle, a few hogs, some horses, some children, and raised a few acres of hay and corn, the barns served as storage space for machinery and shelter for animals. A gambrel roof made more room in the mow for storing hay, which could be pitched to the livestock down below. Fresh air came in through cupolas and hay doors to cool the *(Continued on page 50)*

Flames peel away wheat stubble on the Kansas farm of Albert Skinner. The controlled burn readies the field for planting alfalfa. "Burning helps get rid of insects and weeds fast, but it can cause the soil to wash or blow away," Albert says. "I burn about once every ten years. Normally, I turn stubble under. Keeps the soil in good shape." Sumner County, self-proclaimed "Wheat Capital of the World," produced 15.3 million bushels in 1990. Such abundant harvests draw custom wheat-cutters like the Zirnhelt family (opposite), who bring combines some 700 miles from their farm near Forman, North Dakota, every summer.

*E*yes bright and wise reflect warmth at a traditional feast that includes five generations of Trumbles. Youngest relative Allen Sunde, 3, shoots a mischievous glance at his great-uncle Dwight. This prairie family celebrated Thanksgiving 1990 at Papillion, Nebraska, in the house Dwight Trumble's grandparents built. Opposite, Bette Trumble embraces her husband's great-aunt, Irene Lamb, 98.

FOLLOWING PAGES: Threatening cloud hints at hail, dreaded in Kansas wheat country. Thunderheads can unleash ice pellets that smash the grain crop and, in minutes, wipe out a farmer's yearlong work and potential profits.

flammable hay. In tall, round silos, green fodder was pressed by its own weight—and fermentation—into silage.

Now, as farmers specialize, low-slung, low-maintenance metal sheds are replacing the handsome old barns. But in northern Indiana there survives a type of barn even rarer.

"Well now, round barns," said Shirley Willard, president of the Fulton County Historical Society. "They're mostly in Indiana, Iowa, Illinois, Pennsylvania, and Ohio, but Indiana has the most. There were 225 a few years ago when they were surveyed; now we're down to 115. We lose a few every year." There are only nine in Fulton County, which holds a round-barn festival every summer. That's what Shirley was working on when I found her at the Fulton County Museum.

"Why round barns?" I asked her.

"Many people felt they were more efficient," she said. "The animals all faced the center of the circle, and the farmer had less distance to walk to feed them. And round barns might have been a little easier to keep warm and to maintain. But largely I think it was just a kind of fad. We had a builder here—Kindig & Sons. They promoted round barns and built a lot of them between 1910 and 1924. Would you like to see some of them?"

So we piled into my car and drove through the rich and rolling farmland of Fulton County. Fingers of forest protrude into the prairie here along streams and creeks, and shade trees surround the farmhouses. At the Callaway barn—built in 1915 by the Kindigs, 80 feet in diameter—black-shingle silhouettes of the farm's animals had been worked into a new green roof: a cow, a pig, a sheep, a chicken. The family girls were getting their animals ready for an upcoming fair, hosing down a steer, brushing a lamb. I held Snowball the kitten and tried to stay out of the way. "The man who re-did the roof was really good," said Mrs. Callaway. "He did the design on graph paper. He just kept filling in squares till it looked like a pig. Then a cow, and so forth." It was cool and dark inside the barn, with sparrows in the eaves and cattle in the lower section. The mailbox at the end of the Callaway driveway was a miniature of the round barn—complete down to the animals on its roof.

A few miles away, we found Selena Gerig, 87, eager to talk about her barn as we stood on her shady lawn and admired it. "I was about 11 when it was built. Mother wouldn't allow us children near it while the men were working. She said we'd get in the way. Father picked up all the rocks for the foundation from fields around here. They took the boards down to the creek to soak them so they could be formed into a circle.

"When it was finished we played in it. There was a rope fastened to the rafters, and Dad would swing us on it till we hit the roof. We'd jump into the hay. Now think what that was doing to that hay!"

Selena was shy and gentle, with thin white hair. I complimented her on the neatness of her place. "Thank you. It looks pretty ragged right now. The grass needs cutting. I mowed it myself till three years ago. Now I spend all my time trying to get kids to do it. It was easier to do it myself."

As Shirley and I were getting ready to leave, Selena walked with us to the car. She said, "The saddest thing happened the other day. I feel so bad. I hit a deer with my car! I was starting off for church one evening, just beginning to accelerate, when it leaped in front of me. I didn't see it coming. I didn't hit it very hard. It ran into the woods. But I didn't know what to do. I went on to church, picking up ladies, my friends. I was so ashamed, I didn't even tell them what had happened. I was afraid they wouldn't want to ride with me."

In mid-June, the roadsides were thick with lavender wildflowers that looked like tall clover. As always, it was a relief to get down off the interstates to where I could look the cows in the eye. Down to where I could ease up behind farmers on big green pieces of machinery, inching along, as wide as the highways. Bits of cottonwood fluff floated in my open car windows. The hot weather gave me an excuse to stop often for root-beer floats. At a drive-in I heard the woman in the car beside me say to her husband, "Does it make any damn difference where you get your ice cream?"

I had read that Crown Point, Indiana, had a handsome old courthouse, and when I found it, centered in the town's busy square, renovation was well under way. Begun in 1878, it recently lost its governmental function when county offices moved elsewhere.

"Fifteen years ago there was talk of knocking the courthouse down for a parking lot," said architect Paul Reed, whose firm, IN Architects and Planners Inc., has moved into renovated quarters in the building. "I'd love to see them try. It would have put the wreckers out of business. Some of the foundation walls downstairs are five feet thick. Even up in the clock tower, they're three feet thick." A nonprofit foundation owns the building now and is offering rent-free offices for a few years to firms that will move in and help pay for the renovation.

Paul took me for a tour of the building. "It has an interesting past. Rudolph Valentino, Tom Mix, and Red Grange all got their licenses here and were married in town." It was easy to get married in Crown Point. Justices of the peace were open around-the-clock, and there was no waiting period. So once a couple got a license at the courthouse, they could walk across the square and marry at any hour.

As a town planner, Paul worries about the future of downtowns of small American cities like Crown Point, while malls and strip developments on the outskirts siphon business from the centers. "There are only a few empty buildings in downtown Crown Point, and we're working on getting them filled up. One of the concerns is, people put in little boutiques and specialty shops, but these businesses go through cycles. About every five years they're out of business. You need a better mix. We'd like to get the downtown grocery store back, the hardware store, the drugstore, and even get people living above them again, though the codes forbid that now."

I had missed Crown Point's Festival Days, concluded just a couple of days before. "My kitten got third place in the Pet Parade," said Paul. "First place went to a reptile. Imagine!"

Courthouses, malls, museums—I tried to sample as many as I could. At the mall in Yankton, South Dakota, on a Sunday afternoon, a three-piece polka band—trumpet, drums, accordion—was entertaining a handful of oldsters on folding chairs. The Roger Maris Museum is located in a mall in Fargo, North Dakota: a huge glass case filled with clippings, uniforms, autographed baseballs and bats, trophies. I leaned forward to read a clipping. In high school in Fargo, Roger was a football star; he returned four kickoffs for touchdowns in a single game.

State capitol buildings in the heartland are wide open for exploring. Kansas has one of the nicest, in Topeka. Topeka's namesake railroad—the Atchison, Topeka & Santa Fe—was started in the city in 1869, eight years after Kansas entered the Union. Alf Landon, Republican presidential candidate in 1936, lived here in one of the city's several pleasant, tree-shaded residential sections. The capitol building, modeled after the national capitol, was begun in 1866 but not completed until 1903.

Famous murals by John Steuart Curry attract visitors to the second floor. His tempestuous representation of John Brown in one is often reproduced: Wild-eyed and bushy-haired, Brown is waving a Bible in one hand and a rifle in the other. A prairie fire and a tornado are on the horizon behind him, and dead Civil War soldiers lie at his feet. Not all Kansans approved of the murals when they were painted, and they received a lot of criticism. When Curry did the final touch-up, he added a family of skunks to one mural, because "no Kansas scene would be complete without a skunk." There's a legend that he named each skunk for a critic of his work—the largest one for the governor.

In Lewistown, Illinois, I stumbled onto a celebration commemorating the 75th anniversary of the publication of *Spoon River Anthology*, by Edgar Lee Masters. The little town crouched beneath a fierce sun, and I watched as a thermometer on the corner of a bank clicked from 90° to 91° to 92°. I sat at a picnic table on a church lawn and had a butterfly pork chop sandwich and lemonade as the parade came by. Fire truck, politician, a Model T with members of the Spoon River Professional Women's Club, buggies. The home of the poet's parents was for sale, and I wandered through it. It had been empty for years, so floors sagged and paint peeled. It sold to people who hope to make it into a bed-and-breakfast inn. Masters wrote: "Life all around me here in the village: / Tragedy, comedy, valor and truth, / Courage, constancy, heroism, failure— / All in the loom, and oh what patterns!"

On the car radio, a woman giving the market reports said, "Loins are lower at 1.19. Bellies are firm." I got a more detailed idea about the value of farm animals while touring eastern Illinois with a veterinarian, James Finnell. Dr. Finnell—who graduated from the University of Illinois in 1959 and is universally known in these parts as Doc—is one-third of a three-vet practice in Piper City. "Probably 90 to 95 percent of our work involves farm animals, though the number of small companion animals is growing as people move into our area from the north."

I had first caught up with Doc, 59, at Deckers' Livestock, Inc., an auction market in Milford. He and Glenn Baker, a state animal health inspector, and auctioneer Don Decker were in the lunchroom, where local women were preparing sandwiches and coffee. There was a lot of good-natured joshing. Don said, "Ten years ago, when Dad was living, we used to do our own doctoring until we felt we couldn't save an animal, then we'd call Doc. One day we had three feeder steers that were pretty bad. So Doc came out, and Dad says, 'Whattya think, Doc?' And Doc says, (Continued on page 60)

Grass-roots entrepreneurs: Marty McCabe hammers out a joint venture with Carl and Sarah Barnhart. The trio took in six dollars: the equivalent of about one sale to every ten people in their hometown of New Vienna, Iowa, pop. 376.

FOLLOWING PAGES: *Cranks turn and tongues wag at an ice-cream social near Gladbrook, Iowa. Family ties and church gatherings still bond rural Iowans.*

*N*eighborly ways: Leon Heuer, in cap, greets Jerry Erickson (above) during community days in Enderlin, North Dakota. "As rural America has shrunk, so has our crowd, but we're still going strong," notes Mayor Mitch Rapp. Malea Noennig (opposite) takes to stranger Ellen Herrmann in a farmhouse beauty shop near Norwood, Minnesota. Malea's father accepted Ellen's offer to feed the baby while he tended his son, fretful during his first haircut. In Slater, Missouri, Kathi Rogers chats with Earl Meyer, while Leigh Anne Marsh (left) and Stephanie Thomas form a classic small-town vignette: young people at a soda fountain.

*P*oking good-natured fun at your opponent figures in the strategy of dominoes played in the back rooms of prairie-town stores. Jim Buckle and Wayne New share the laughter as Rick Howard (center) and retired sheriff Jay Brown (right) tease Phil Piersol during a game in Williamsburg, Kansas. Appropriately, they wear baseball caps. Headgear tells whether a person belongs to the plains or to the prairies. Ranchers wear cowboy hats; farmers wear caps, which often bear the names and logos of farm machinery or co-op organizations. Such makeshift domino parlors in small communities serve as social centers where friends can meet and chew the fat. Topics include the weather, farming, and the latest goings-on in town. These cronies lost their table space when the seed and produce store closed. The owner was forced out of business because "the little towns are disintegrating, and that's what happened."

'I think I can save two out of three.' Dad says, 'That'd be great.' Next week Doc was here, and Dad says, 'Doc, you're battin' a thousand.' Doc says, 'They all live?' And Dad says, 'No, they all died.' "

I watched Doc in action back in the pens behind the auction ring. With a syringe in each hand, he stepped into a pen churning with piglets. He would straddle a pig from behind, hold it snug with his knees, time his move carefully, then quickly jab a needle behind each ear. Talk about a stuck pig! They shrieked like preschoolers getting shots.

I asked Doc about changes in veterinary medicine since he's been practicing. "It used to be we mostly put out fires—dealt with emergencies of one kind or another. Now it's largely preventative medicine. In some cases, we're on a consulting basis with farmers. I'll visit a farm maybe once a month, go over their records, talk about any disease problems, teach them to administer vaccines, and so forth. That's different. And we're seeing some different animals around, a few llamas. A llama is like a horse in a cow's body. They have expressive eyes.

"Here at the auction, if breeding cattle change hands, I pull a blood sample from them, test it for brucellosis, and send it to Springfield to be double-checked. Brucellosis, pseudorabies, tuberculosis—we check for these things, give shots and castrate pigs, examine any animal that looks sick."

I joined Glenn, the animal health inspector, in the stands and watched some cattle and hogs being sold. A couple of hundred seats faced a sawdust arena backed by an elevated auctioneer's booth, manned by Don and two or three helpers. Now 77, Glenn had farmed until he was 69, while his wife taught school.

"You're probably seeing here the passing of a segment of American agriculture," he mused. "As farmers get more specialized, raising just cattle or just hogs, they market direct to the slaughterhouses, bypassing places like this. As the small farmer disappears, these places disappear, and as these places disappear, the small farmer disappears.

"Many people around here are grain farmers. They won't have a head of stock on the place, just big fields of corn or beans. Maybe 2,000 acres and not a hoof of livestock. Not even a chicken. When I was farming, farms were diversified. Every time you went to town, you'd buy a little something. A few nails, some chicken feed. Now you don't need anything. That's what's ruining these little towns."

About 30 men sat in the stands, some with calculators. It was difficult to detect the movements that registered bids, so I sat very still. First in were 70 head of 40-pound hogs, pink and white, a wave of frantic squealing. They went for $44 a head. These were feeder pigs; farmers would take them home and fatten them up for market, then bring them back to be sold again when they were ready to be butchered.

Later I moved a little higher in the stands and found myself near Kip Harms, who looked too young to be a farmer. "This is my first year," he told me. "I graduated last year from Illinois State University in Bloomington with a major in agriculture production. I brought ten cattle over to sell today. They're not great, but they're not going to get any better, just fatter. If I fed them another couple of months, I wouldn't get any more for them."

Kip relies on a marketing service to advise him on buying and selling. "You can't go broke if you don't lose money," he says. He doesn't eat at places that he thinks may buy beef from South America.

The first of Kip's steers into the ring caused quite a commotion. A big, belligerent crossbreed weighing 750 pounds, it thundered into the ring, tail up, head swiveling, looking for a fight. To everyone's consternation it got its front feet up into the auctioneer's booth, then lurched and heaved itself all the way in, practically into Don Decker's lap. He went over backward, and people scrambled out of the way. Someone opened a door and herded the steer back into the ring, where it stood, glaring defiantly, ready for another fight. "In 45 years," said Don, when things had quieted down, "that's the first time that's happened."

"Do cows bite?" I asked Kip.

He looked at me askance. "Cows don't have upper front teeth, so they can't bite," he said. "Anyway, they'd rather step on you than bite you. And they'd rather knock you down than step on you."

"Will you miss the ones you're selling?"

"You don't miss individual cows," he said. "You miss the routine of taking care of them."

I accompanied Doc on visits to a couple of local farms. One raised cattle, the other hogs. Vernon Veatch, in his 70s, his son Ryan, and his grandsons Bryan and Brad raise cattle near Roberts, Illinois. Courtly and quiet, Vernon walked me past pens full of cattle that stood coolly chewing their cuds, watching us go by.

The Veatches buy cattle that have been living in pastures eating grass and already weigh between 600 and 650 pounds. "Then we bring them here and put the marble to them," said Vernon. "We make 'em edible. What you're trying to do is get your animal up to, say, 1,100 pounds and not get too much fat on him. People are buying extra-lean these days." The Veatches feed their cattle a mixture of silage—which they make themselves, chopping corn they grow on the farm—and gluten, with a little nitrogen added. "That's the thing about a ruminant," said Doc. "They can take elemental nitrogen and make protein."

"We sell maybe 50 cattle a week," said Vernon, "all year round, which helps avoid the hazard of having to sell when the market is down."

"You could brush these guys off and take 'em to the fair," said Doc.

Doc and I headed for a hog operation a few miles away, with a stop for coffee. "If I don't have some coffee in the middle of the afternoon," Doc said, "I stop talking."

At Lehmann Farms, Art Lehmann and Robert Frase, the herdsman, zipped me into coveralls and boots, and walked me through several long, low buildings resounding to the grunting, oinking, snorting, squealing, and snoring of thousands of pigs. There were pigs of every size—from pink, hairless toddlers born that day to grande dame matrons pregnant with their fourth or fifth litter. The farm's goal is much like that of the Veatches—to tightly control all aspects of a pig's life, from birth to market, and to have pigs ready to sell each week, to catch the average price.

"We work on a weekly schedule," said Robert, as we stood looking over a shed full of hogs. "These sows are all ready to farrow"—which meant they were extremely pregnant. "Little pigs stay with their mothers three weeks and are weaned on Mondays and Thursdays. A sow whose piglets are weaned on Thursday will be back in heat on Monday—so she's taken to the breeding barn on Monday and bred."

Ingenious pens gave piglets room to get away from the sows, to avoid being crushed. "You need to keep your preweaning mortality down," said Robert. "We lose an average of 0.7 pig per litter," Art added. "The problem is you have a 3-pound baby and a 350- or 400-pound mother."

"When people talk about pork belly futures, this is what they're talking about," said Doc. "Bacon."

In another building, newborn piglets were cute, but undeniably pigs. They were getting an iron shot, their tails docked, their canine teeth clipped so they couldn't damage a teat, and a code snipped into their ears. Another building had young pigs that had been weaned. They were being fed a rich mixture—pellets, and whey discarded from a cheese factory in Champaign. "You want them to leave a little food so you'll know they're not going hungry," said Robert. Little toys hung down over the pigs for them to play with. Each building has an alarm. "If the temperature drops, phones start ringing all over the county," said Doc.

In another barn I got a look at two purebred Hampshire boars—Wally and his other brother Wally, named in a nod to the Bob Newhart Show—which do the begetting. And finally, in the finishing house, pigs reach a weight of about 230 pounds, and then they're sold.

Earlier, at Deckers' Livestock, Kip had mentioned that his hometown, Cullom, was about to hold its annual fair. "Stop by if you get a chance," he said. I like fairs, so I did.

Cullom, in eastern Illinois, is a town of fewer than 600 people. *You can't throw dirt without losin' a little ground,* sang the radio as I looked for it,

Costumed to compete in the 114th annual Ponca Powwow at White Eagle, Oklahoma, dancer Danny Page wears a traditional porcupine-quill hair roach. Powwows, part homecoming, part ritual, reaffirm Native American identity.

barely missing some pheasants gliding across the highway. Around here you can spot little towns from a distance by their thick tree cover. They straddle the highway, and railroad tracks run past the grain elevator. A gas station, a roadside café, perhaps a drive-in—they look interchangeable, but rivalries between high schools can be fierce.

Cullom's Main Street was aglitter with carnival, and the town park, at the end of the street, was full of tents of penned sheep, hogs, and cattle.

A middle-aged couple in jeans with matching belts walked by, holding hands, and a farmer's cap read "Midwest Computer Supply." A little girl showing her pig got tangled up with another one and fell down in the sawdust. It didn't hurt her, only embarrassed her. She cried and went to her father on the sidelines for a hug. Later, in the cattle tent, I overheard two girls grooming their entrants. "I use Prell on the white parts of Herefords," one said. "It really whitens them. Then I use a vinegar solution to get the soap out. It cuts down on dandruff."

Fairs of all sizes can be found throughout the prairie states all summer long, and I attended as many as I could. In Washington, Missouri, the Town and Country Fair, slightly larger than Cullom's, was held during five days in early August. A recent rain had sent the humidity soaring. In the show ring, junior-high girls with braces on their teeth were being yanked around by huge steers. One was named Big Matt.

In the hog barn I found the grand champion pig, a 292-pound mixed Duroc-Hampshire shown by Ben Tobben, 8, and named Cindy, "for my sister." Cindy the sister was "tickled pink," according to her mother, to have such a successful namesake. I sought refuge from the humidity in the beer tent and listened for a while to a fiddlers' contest. Later I strolled through the midway, eating a corn dog with mustard. "That was a rough ride," I heard a little girl tell her father, after being sick on the Tilt-A-Whirl. As the afternoon ended, I sat with several thousand others on a hillside and listened to Ronnie Milsap—one of the fair's star country music attractions.

The Douglas County 4-H/FFA fair at Lawrence, Kansas, is another step up in size from Cullom. Lawrence has a population of about 65,000 and is home to the University of Kansas. It was an abolitionist stronghold before and during the Civil War. The Confederate bushwhacker William C. Quantrill staged a famous guerrilla raid here in August 1863, massacring 150 men and boys and looting and burning the town.

I visited the fair on a lovely August morning. Isaac Ulrich, 11, from Baldwin City, was tending his rabbits in the rabbit barn. He had shown the reserve champion mini-lop. "That means it was almost the best," he said. Some rabbits were enjoying what someone called rabbit air-conditioning: large plastic soft-drink bottles filled with water and frozen, against which the rabbits sprawl.

In the sheep barn, somebody was wearing a T-shirt that read "I Love Ewe." Many of the animals had on smocks to keep them clean. It made them look like doctors. Organized chaos reigned in the pig arena, with a couple of dozen pigs milling around being tended by children with switches. The goats, on the other hand, were well behaved but stubborn. One little boy, number 185, knelt beside his and kissed it on the nose. The goats had choke chains around their necks to control them.

Kim Prager, a self-possessed 13, had won three grand champion ribbons, two second place ribbons, and about seven first places. "Your goats look smart," I said. "Are they?"

Prairie van Gogh, artist Stan Herd zigzags a tractor to etch his "Sunflower Still Life." Soybeans and clover made up most of the 20-acre image near Eudora, Kansas. Actual sunflowers, the state's official flower, formed the bright blooms.

LARRY FLEMING

"Pretty smart," she said. "Smarter than stuff like sheep."

The Clay County Fair in Spencer, Iowa, bills itself as the world's greatest county fair, and it may be. Certainly it's big. It runs eight days, and big-name entertainers perform—in 1990 Tanya Tucker, the Charlie Daniels Band, the Statler Brothers, the Judds.

It's hot in Iowa in September but cool in the barns, with an earthy smell. Huge fans keep the air moving for two or three people sitting around in lawn chairs. Somebody is grooming a cow, and somebody else is bringing a bucket of water. A teenage girl is wearing Holstein earrings. Cows rest demurely with their feet folded under them like cats. They nod their heads when they walk, I note, and it's difficult to know what they're thinking. Pigs sprawl on their sides as if shot. They care solely about sleeping. Only lambs seem to have personalities.

Outside, the bingo caller's cry—"N fourteen. O sixty-one"—blended with the clatter of iron on iron from the horseshoe pitch. Five elderly ladies stood in a circle, trying to decide where to eat. "I don't care," said one. "I don't care either," said another. "Well I certainly don't care," said a third. Immobilized by courtesy. At afternoon's end, two identical twin boys, toddlers dressed identically, threw identical tantrums, crying in perfect harmony, as artful as the Judds. In the parking lot, attendants on horseback directed cars to the exits.

The Iowa State Fair in Des Moines is almost too big. I entered the gate, checked my program, and despaired of ever seeing everything. Whenever I couldn't decide what to do next, I ate. In two days I had two hot dogs on sticks, ice cream on a stick, a Polish sausage sandwich, a sausage grinder, a Maid Rite hamburger, an apple dumpling with ice cream, popcorn, three Cokes, numerous coffees.

I saw barnacle geese and broody shells, a kind of duck. On the Avenue of Breeds I saw Chinese pigs, an albino catfish, a llama, an ostrich, a Texas longhorn, a pot-bellied pig from Vietnam, and learned that a Brangus is five-eighths Angus and three-eighths Brahman. The pigeon barn had more kinds of pigeons than you would think possible: homers, which were subdivided into young cocks and old hens, old cocks and young hens; Mookees; Komorners; Ices—the variety with feet like huge feathered snowshoes; Franconian Trumpeters; Chinese Owls; English Carriers that looked like buzzards. There were Fantails with huge peacock-like tails, and round, chubby Red Gazzi Modenas.

I watched a judge judge some beautiful vegetables: cabbages, carrots, onions, potatoes, squash, pumpkins, ear corn, kohlrabi. Of the kohlrabi, the woman beside me said, "You can eat it raw. It's kind of crunchy like the heart of a cabbage, only not so hard." Bart Simpson was on about every tenth chest.

I saw a Jersey black giant rooster in a cage crow right into the face of a flabbergasted toddler.

Cattle exhibitors had long switches for tickling their cows' bellies as they showed them, to keep them calm. The grand champion Angus bull looked like a stealth tugboat, all muscle. The best-of-show dollhouse had a cat asleep on the porch and birds at the birdfeeder. Even antiques were judged. In the pig arena, Miss Duroc, a pretty girl in high heels, wobbled through the sawdust to present the ribbons.

The judges amazed me. They would examine painstakingly a score of animals, line them up in the order of their excellence, then take a hand microphone and run down the line, pointing out each animal's good and bad points. I paid attention when one finished judging a group of lambs, and this is part of what he said: "We're going to start off with a very lean kind of a lamb, one that's extremely hard and firm. The young lady does a good job of getting all the mileage she can out of it. A very straight-topped kind of a sheep, one that comes out very level and square, as I say, handles very hard and firm all the way through. We might have some lambs in this class that have just a notch more muscle back through their legs, but, a fairly thick muscled kind of a lamb, and along with the leanness he displays, we feel we can justify him on top today.

"Second place, a lamb you really don't appreciate, we kind of lost him for a while and didn't find him until about the middle of the class, but when you start analyzing, again, a big old long-topped lamb. He's got some top to him and some muscle, some bulge up there; the lamb has just a little less middle to him, he's a little shrunk up today. I'd like to see him a little fuller than he is, so the lamb logically falls into second."

And so on down through ten sheep. "The lamb in fifth place is a little open-shouldered in my mind, but a very competitive lamb in his own right . . . . and in tenth, our last purple today, a lamb that just doesn't have quite as much shape down his top as some of the other lambs. A good class. Thank you."

Practically every little town in the prairie has a museum nowadays, and whenever I saw a sign on the highway pointing toward one, I'd stop for a few minutes. One disturbing discovery: Artifacts from my youth are beginning to show up in museums. The Buffalo Gap Historic Village Museum in Texas included in its collection a kind of soft-drink machine that you found at gas stations when I was growing up. You put your money in, opened a round metal door, and were presented with a bottle—a *bottle*—of pop lying on its side, its cap toward you. With a clatter and (Continued on page 74)

FOLLOWING PAGES: *Sticky, sweaty, itchy job of unloading wheat at a grain elevator eases up long enough for Brian Klein to rest. He works the summer harvest to earn college money. In a few minutes another semitrailer will lumber in from fields around Garden Plain, Kansas. Most wheat towns sprang up around grain elevators, which rise like prairie castles above the landscape.*

*R*ural road makes a beeline past rows of corn and grain bins on the Dan
Beane farm in Marshall County, Iowa. Across the road Dan raises soybeans,
which he weeds with a cultivator. One of Iowa's Century Farms—land that has
belonged to one family for more than a hundred years—the property was
purchased by Dan's great-grandfather in 1875. Iowa's unusually fertile soil yields
more than a billion bushels of corn and 300 million bushels of soybeans annually.

*F*irst woman elected principal chief, Wilma Mankiller (above) presides over
the Cherokee nation, headquartered in Tahlequah, Oklahoma. The state takes pride
in its 67 Indian tribes and its oil. Black gold made the city of Tulsa an oil capital;
today its skyline rises above the Arkansas River (below), in view of storage tanks
owned by the Sun Company. The firm helps support Street School, Inc., an
alternative education program for high school dropouts. Teacher Robert Anderson
and student Annie Leach, both Cherokee, confer in a computer science class.

bang, you pulled it out. It reminded me that, in terms of European settlement, the prairie's past is a short one, the merest tail end of recorded history. In the prairie, something a hundred years old is ancient.

At the Manitoba Museum of Man and Nature in Winnipeg, you're greeted just inside the door by a terrific diorama: a huge, wild-eyed bison coming right at you about to be shot with a rifle by a Métis hunter on horseback. Farther inside, there's an alarming model of a mosquito as big as a small chicken, and a clump of crested wheatgrass mounted on the wall; its roots dangle eight feet.

Several museums display sod houses, and Winnipeg's has a sign: "The sod house provided good insulation from the cold, the heat, and the wind of the western interior. Rain was another thing. It was often said that if it rained outside for a day it would surely rain inside for two."

The Truman Library Museum in Independence, Missouri, showed a '41 Chrysler he owned, as well as the flag that was raised over Berlin on July 4, 1945. Several of the women visitors looked like Bess Truman. In the courtyard, a carillon softly chimed.

President Truman's library is only a few miles east of the Kansas City metropolis, fourth largest of the heartland's urban areas (after Chicago, St. Louis, and Minneapolis-St. Paul). Kansas Citians are Missourians or Kansans by virtue of a boundary that winds along in the Missouri River and then strikes south along a thoroughfare named State Line Road; but for statistical and other purposes the two cities amount to one. Lying only 257 miles from the geographic center of the 48 contiguous states—which is 39°50' North, 98°35' West, in Smith County, Kansas—the city has used its pivotal location to become a transportation and marketing hub. Grain futures change hands at a frantic pace at the Board of Trade. I paused briefly at a city park on high ground where Lewis and Clark stood on September 15, 1806. They deemed it an ideal site for a fort because of its perfect command of the rivers. Gazing northward across the Kansas River to Kaw Point, I could see freeway cloverleafs and warehouses, as well as the confluence of the Kansas and Missouri Rivers.

Just west of the urban sprawl, at the entrance to the Agricultural Hall of Fame, I found two doors side by side. A sign on one said: "Please Use West Door." Typical of farmers; anybody else would have said, "Please Use Other Door." The hall displayed portraits and short biographies of famous personages: John Deere, Henry Agard Wallace, Eli Whitney.

I was interested in the comments of a group of Amish farmers wandering through, looking at the exhibits, but they were shy and spoke softly, and their accents baffled me.

Downstairs a re-created prairie town evoked the good old days, from the 1860s to the 1930s: a harness shop, an undertaker, a vet, I. L. Pullem the dentist. Frankly I'd rather have trusted my luck to the vet than Dr. Pullem, whose equipment looked like medieval torture instruments.

The most interesting museums in the prairie were often the ones with the fewest cars in the lot. In west-central Minnesota I found one with *no* cars in the lot, just the proprietor's pickup. Arnold Leaderbrand, 69, was in charge that day at the Finn Creek Open Air Museum, and he dropped what he was doing to show me around.

Neat and tidy farms in this vicinity produce beef and dairy products, and alfalfa hay, oats, corn, and soybeans. By 1890, there were nearly 500,000 immigrants living in Minnesota, about one-third of the total population. All but 35,000 of the foreign-born were of German, Scandinavian, or English-speaking origin. Between 1880 and 1890, the Scandinavians were the most numerous of the immigrants.

Finn Creek Museum now claims 18 acres of the 80 that Siffert and Wilhelmiina Tapio settled in 1900. The house and a sauna are original, and other farm buildings have been brought in and filled with artifacts used by Finnish settlers. Arnold started me off on my tour in the farmhouse. A handsome stove in the kitchen made me whistle. "Donated by Lester Kasma, 1915," its label read. Arnold picked up the kettle from it. "I'm seven months older than this kettle. Mother scratched the date on it, see there? November 1921. I was born in April. This reservoir on the stove kept water warm. In winter, the teakettle sang all the time." A coffee grinder, a rug beater, a cream separator, cream cans.

"My dad settled in this county as an auctioneer in 1917. Came here from Illinois. He spoke seven languages, Norwegian until he went to school, then English.

"This was the living room in the daytime, a bedroom at night." He pulled out a rollaway bed. "I always say that's why these Finns had so many children; once you got your wife in there, she couldn't get away." An aside to me: "You have to know who you can say certain things to." An old Finnish Bible, open to the 21st Psalm. Sewing machines. Spectacles.

"It's always fun to see old places like this," I said.

"You betcha," said Arnold.

Arnold showed me how to hoist a bucket of water with the sweep at the well, showed me the saunas, with oak switches still in place, showed me the summer kitchen. We walked out toward one of the barns. "The lady who took care of me, she was a midwife. Dad got her at night and she'd forgot her pipe; she smoked an old corncob pipe. So Dad gave her a cigar. She's in an elders' home now. I walk in to see her and she yells, 'My baby!' *(Continued on page 80)*

FOLLOWING PAGES: Long summer shadows darken combine tracks and highlight the windrow pattern in a harvested Iowa oat field. Straw tailings left from the threshing fleck the golden rows. Seeded in late March under a protective cover of oats, alfalfa emerges with a verdant tinge to contribute to next year's crop in the cycle of planting, growth, and harvest vital to farmsteads in the heartland.

*S*tructurally sound, a lean kind of lamb, well muscled, good breeding stock: Such points impress judges and may produce winners for these 4-H and FFA youngsters who hold their ewe lambs in line. Livestock judging heralded the 109th Clark County Fair in Kahoka, Missouri. Traditionally, agricultural fairs serve as teaching grounds and showcases for farmers of all ages. Some participants, such as 5-year-old Emily Sederburg (right), stand hardly taller than their show animals, in this case, Sam the lamb. Emily entered Sam in the fair's market competition, which made him eligible for auction. He earned Emily $95.

"I'm gonna turn you loose in here and go put that coffeepot on." An old Remington typewriter with Finnish characters. Snowshoes. Oxen shoes. A scythe with a cradle. Many of the artifacts had been donated by Arnold. "I think I could fill this building with just my own stuff." Birch skis 15 feet long. A bear trap, welded open. A sled made out of barrel staves. A tool for digging potatoes. An incubator for baby chicks. "The doggone women were supposed to be here today labeling this stuff." A bean grader. A broadax.

We talked some more over coffee and cookies. "My old neighbor says the Germans came in here and cut the timber off and left us with the rocks and the stumps. I remember plowing pine roots up."

Arnold served as a merchant seaman during World War II. "I went 7 times to France, 14 times to England. We had sub attacks. When they dropped depth charges, the whole ship would shake. Murmansk in winter—now that was something. We hauled troops home after the war. I went twice through the Panama Canal. The best cement work I ever saw was in that canal. I was ready to fight when they gave it away."

A museum I visited in Illinois is at the center of a controversy. The Dickson Mounds Museum, on a bluff along the Illinois River, displays the exposed burials of 237 Indians. The site was excavated by archaeologist Don Dickson, who opened his museum in 1927; it was bought by the state in 1945.

Many Native Americans say the exhibit is disrespectful of their ancestors and want it closed. While I was in Illinois, then Governor James R. Thompson considered the matter and announced that the museum would remain open. The next morning a headline read: "Violence Is Hinted Over Tribal Graves." Members of an Indian organization had threatened to close the museum themselves. So I drove over to have a look.

Everything was peaceful and quiet. There were tourists with cameras, tour buses, sunshine, and birdsong. It *is* a macabre display. It's as if someone had dug down six feet in a cemetery and left the bones lying where they were found—limbs akimbo, jaws agape, the skeletons of babies snug against their mothers, remains in some cases piled one atop another.

I asked Dan Wildcat about it. A Yuchi Indian, Dan teaches sociology at Haskell Indian Junior College in Lawrence, Kansas. "The Smithsonian Institution has recently adopted a policy for returning the remains of American Indians to the tribes for burial," he said. "I think it's time the people at Dickson Mounds were allowed to rest in peace."

Now an accredited junior college with 41 buildings on a 320-acre campus, Haskell began in 1884 as an elementary school for Indian children and evolved through periods as a high school and later as a vocational-technical school. Some 800 students attend from more than 100 tribes all over the country. "We're much like any other junior college," Dan said, as we sat in his cluttered office, "with two exceptions. First, we're a community college, but our community is huge. It takes in the whole country. I hope before too long we'll be able to drop the junior from our name and become an accredited four-year college. Second, as an Indian college, we strive to foster a sense of respect and pride in our history and cultural heritage.

"Anyone who's a member of a federally recognized tribe, or who can show descent from a recognized tribe, can attend here tuition free, with free housing and meals." He thought about that for a second. "It's not really *free*, of course. A lot was given up to get that right.

"We get students of all kinds here. Many don't have the kind of self-confidence you'd like to see. They arrive feeling that because they're Indians they shouldn't expect to go to college, shouldn't expect to succeed or do well. This can result in more problems. Some teachers here have what we call 'the missionary complex.' They really want to help, but they think, 'It's not fair to expect these Indian kids to do as well as whites,' so they lower their standards and pave the way for the students to fail when they matriculate in predominantly white colleges and universities.

"I went to the University of Kansas here in Lawrence. I taught there for a while, and I've had students here say to me, 'You act like we're students at KU.' And I say, 'You're right. That's exactly the way I act.'

"American Indians have been taught to be contemptuous of their culture." He pulled a book off a shelf. "This is *History of the United States of America* by Henry William Elson, a 1918 copy. Listen." He read from "The Indian," chapter two. " 'He followed the dictates of his conscience . . . which was based on tribal custom and not upon religion, [while it] bade him to be honest and kind in his dealings with his own people, it permitted him to steal from his enemy, to destroy his property, and to torture him to death.' Or this, about the home life of the Indian. 'It was scarcely above that of the animals that inhabited the forest. . . . He lived in a den of filth. . . .' We probably had students reading this. Or this. 'We have read of the Indian wars of colonial days—of the horrible massacres, the inhuman tortures; of the bands of hideous warriors who roamed over hills and valleys, seeking out the peaceful abode of the industrious pioneer'—I'm not making this up—'who, with his devoted wife and loving children, had sought to make a home in the wilderness. . . .' " Dan slammed the book shut.

After lunch, we toured the campus, visiting the sports complex, the print shop, classrooms—and a poignant cemetery on one edge of the campus. "I like to bring people here. It represents something we shouldn't forget. These are the graves of children who died here. When Haskell was started, one solution to the 'Indian problem' was to bring children here and, in effect, turn them into whites. Imagine, having your children forcibly taken from you, taken maybe a thousand miles away, not allowed to speak their language, *punished* for speaking their language, and keeping them here for years.

"These children died of childhood diseases. The flu. We forget that people used to die of the flu. The students who come here today may be

Arms raised to heaven in praise, Carson Ford surrenders to the power of prayer as the Reverend Carl Rosin speaks in tongues and asks for divine healing through the laying on of hands. Fellow worshipers offer their devout support during this "restoration revival" in the Red Fourkiller Amphitheater near Stilwell, Oklahoma. Mr. Rosin is an evangelist of Free Holiness, an offshoot of the Pentecostal Protestant movement. The evangelists and their followers hold services that feature forceful preaching, lively singing, and exorcism.

homesick and unhappy, but they come by choice, and there's little danger of them dying. If they think they've got it rough, they should think about these children."

We strolled along, reading headstones. There was a generator humming nearby. A silent jet made a contrail high overhead. "Antonio Prieto, 1911, died at 16. Thomas Little Wolf, 1908, 11 years old, Sioux. He was a long way from home, either North or South Dakota. Here's a Navajo. Often the cavalry was involved in rounding up these children and bringing them here. A Cheyenne. Winnebago. They came from all over. Hopi. Here's a Chippewa. I think of this as truly sacred ground."

Dan put me in touch with Henry T. Collins, 49, a Ponca Indian who worked in law enforcement before becoming one of the security guards at the college. Henry's fame as a singer and drummer of traditional Indian music is nationwide. I found him in the rec room of his home stringing beads at a card table. A large man with a handsome mustache, he spoke in a deep and resonant voice, and softly. He put the beads aside, offered me a glass of tea, and talked with me about Indian music.

"A Plains Indian warrior stood before the tribe or council reciting his deeds and accomplishments while slowly tapping on his war shield with his bow," he said. "From this evolved drumming and singing as we know it today, songs of different kinds—of war, of travel, of happiness. I got interested as a little boy. When I was seven or eight, I began to notice the costumes and the dancing. We children would dance out behind the tents or the bleachers." I was surprised to learn that, while many Indian songs are hundreds of years old, others are being written today. "Many are written by veterans coming out of the service. Most are just melodies; no words."

Henry spoke of his drums with the reverence others might feel for a religious artifact, and used the phrase "the spirit of the drum" perhaps half a dozen times during our talk. "Each drum has a spirit—the way you might refer to the spirit of a man. Singers around a drum invoke that spirit. If you look at a dance arena from above, the drum is in the center, like an altar. People dance clockwise around it, like the movement of the universe. Singers have to humble themselves before the drum before they touch it; they make offerings to it and pray. If you're not in the right spirit, you can't conjure up the spirit of the drum."

Indians from many tribes gather for powwows today. Henry is among the most sought-after leaders of the singing because he knows the other tribes' songs, knows which are appropriate to which ceremony, knows

Hobo on holiday, Frisco Jack freshens up for the annual Hobo Convention in Britt, Iowa. Today very few of the 20,000 attendees qualify as genuine hoboes, migratory workers who rode the rails in America's heartland and beyond.

how to ask permission of another tribe to sing one of its songs. His travels with the drum take him all over the country.

"The drum has been good to me. Everything I have today I owe to the drum, that spirit. My children are healthy and humble. The traveling I've done, the knowledge I've gained—I attribute it to the drum."

Is his knowledge of Indian music being passed on? "Indians are noted for being patient. Not kids today. They're used to getting what they want right now.

"They have no knowledge of how to fix their costumes or drums properly; they can't understand their own heritage. The kids today don't know how to identify costumes with tribes. They should glorify their own tribal heritage. Instead, they will wear another tribe's costume without obtaining the proper permission and blessing from that tribe. I feel kind of bad. They say they want to learn, but they don't understand that it takes years to learn ritual and singing and dancing. They don't understand how profound and beautiful their pasts are."

The past is a presence throughout the prairie, and I found it in a number of places, including the domain of Ermadene Dickey, who with her husband, Art, runs the Greteman General Store at Living History Farms near Des Moines. The Dickeys took on the Greteman project a decade ago. They dress in period clothes and answer visitors' questions and show off the store's extensive collection of antique goods—the sorts of things that would have been found in a general store in 1875. Ermadene laid some of the old implements on the counter and challenged the visitors to identify them. "This is the one nobody ever guesses," she said. It looked like a big metal hacksaw with the blade removed. "I offer peppermint sticks to anyone who can guess it. I've only given two away. And both of them were to tool collectors. See? It was to raise a buggy to grease the wheel. You took the nut off the hub, see? And these threads went up against the hub. This went through the spokes to the axle, so you had the leverage then to raise the buggy, pull the wheel over, grease it, put it back. Isn't that something?

"This other"—a kind of big funnel—"was for giving medicine to a horse. My husband says he'll never have distemper because he drank more medicine than his horse did when he tried to dose it with a long-necked bottle. These were early sunglasses; we found that smoked lenses go back to 1846." Ermadene and Art had first made a hobby of old general stores. "Not many left now," said Ermadene. She tried to pass off a tall tale with a straight face: "Now this, this is an ear trumpet. My husband sold one to a man who said he hadn't heard a thing his wife had said for 25 years, and two days later he brought it back, said he'd heard all he wanted. Now I don't believe that at all, I don't care."

As I traveled through the heartland, I watched for anything with the word "prairie" attached to it. For instance, Fargo, North Dakota, broadcasts Prairie Public Television, and from Bismarck, North Dakota, comes "Prairie Things Considered" on Prairie Public Radio.

In Winnipeg it was the *Prairie Dog Central,* one of Canada's last steam trains. Winnipeg—60 miles north of the U.S. at the confluence of the Red and the Assiniboine Rivers—was the portal through which thousands of immigrants reached Canada's prairie provinces. Many made the city their home, giving it a cosmopolitan air. Among its chief businesses are slaughtering hogs and meat-packing (including turkey products) and trading grain commodity futures.

The *Prairie Dog Central* makes two excursions each Sunday in the summer from Winnipeg to Grosse Isle, Manitoba, and back, giving visitors an opportunity to see what turn-of-the-century train travel was like. "Just sit down, Father. You'll end up getting left behind," a wife warned her husband, who was contemplating getting off to take a photo of the train before we left. Our route out of Winnipeg took us along the rear of businesses: Wendy's, Fanny's Fabrics, West End Upholsterers. It was a cool day and overcast, and a chilly breeze found its way in. The fire in a coal stove at the front of the car felt good. "Ladies and gentlemen, boys and girls. . .," the conductor would say, calling our attention to something. A jackrabbit sat beside the tracks, and a fox loped through the golden stubble of a field that was dotted with bales of hay. The wife was now explaining the camera to her husband: "With this you get wide. Scenery." Wide it was, the vista through which we rolled. Wheat fields and pastures stretched to the horizon, flatter than the prairies farther south. This was no rolling ocean of grass, but a placid lake.

In Swift Current, Saskatchewan, "prairie" on a flyer caught my eye: "Come and Meet Author Bob Waldon who will be autographing his book *A Prairie Guide to Feeding Winter Birds* at Coles the book people! Wheatland Mall." I found him there at a small table, with a stack of books beside him, discussing goldfinches. "Usually we don't have any, but this year there were lots." I bought a copy of Bob's book and learned that goldfinches can tolerate temperatures of minus 94°F if they have sufficient food to maintain a critical level of body fat. "There are other books about feeding birds in winter," Bob told me, "but most are American. And winter in, say, West Virginia is very different from here." "How *do* birds survive these awful Canadian winters," I asked him. "Many don't. Kinglets die by the thousand. They're so tiny you wonder how they can live at all. They weigh sixteen-hundredths of an ounce; it takes a hundred of them to make a pound. Seen next to a kinglet, a chickadee looks positively hulking."

In Kansas a roadside sign stopped me: Pretty Prairie. A cold, rainy wind was blowing as I turned toward the town. Cows stood in a huddle in a corner of a field with their backs to the wind. It looked as if they were all watching something interesting in the next field. *(Continued on page 92)*

*P*rairie fun: Tossing its "pieces" in flips, a lawn-chair drill team delights
Fourth of July parade watchers in Independence, Iowa. Fire-hose teams duel in
nearby Rowley. The pair that propels the water ball across a white line wins.

FOLLOWING PAGES: *Proud banner boosts the Academy football team in Spalding,
Nebraska. Safe streets in many prairie towns allow youngsters like Travis and
Samantha Ray to shop on their own and fetch home a wagonload of groceries.*

SHAMROCKS

Toddling cuties in fancy dress experience a heartland tradition: the beauty contest. Anna Christine Campbell, turning her back on the judges, won first place. Crystal Kearney took third at the 1990 Volkfest in Slater, Missouri.

Pretty Prairie has about 600 people, a main street, and some lovely old maples on Maple Street. In the downtown café, old-timers were trying to top one another's ailments. "Doc told me last week," said one, "a diabetic's body age is his age plus the number of years he's been taking insulin. That makes me 130 years old." This momentarily silenced his companions. The talk turned then to cockleburs and coon hunting. A UPS truck went past. I heard somebody mention Bob Collins's new baby buffalo, so next day I located Bob, who keeps a herd of 20 head or so. He loaded me into his pickup and took me to his farm to see the youngster. Three days old, it was as cute as you might expect. It stuck close to its mother's shaggy knees, a paler shade of brown. "Watch out if a bison's tail comes up," said Bob. "It means trouble."

He showed me through the big house where he lives alone with a timorous dog. "My wife's got the Alzheimer's. It's been a year since she knew me." Downstairs were artifacts from a lifetime. Old sidesaddles, bows and arrows, longhorn horns, a saw used by the gangs that butchered buffalo for the railroad crews, fossils, branding irons. Bob is the third generation of his family on the ranch, and it will be five if one of his two grandsons takes it over. One is studying commercial art in Atlanta, the other forestry at Kansas State. "It just goes to show," said Bob, "They were raised within a year of each other right here, but they couldn't be more different."

Bob's routine seldom varies. In the morning, he goes to town, drinks coffee in the café, plays cards, comes back to the farm to do whatever needs doing, then goes back to town to eat. In the afternoons, he visits his wife.

For many years there's been talk of a prairie park over to the east, where the Flint Hills preserve the largest remnant of tallgrass prairie. In Council Grove, which calls itself a "Rendezvous on the Santa Fe Trail," I got wind of it again. Council Grove issues a walking-tour map of itself that features a number of historic attractions: the Old Calaboose; the Madonna of the Trail, a monument honoring pioneer women; the Custer Elm, a stubby remnant where the general bought some land; the trunk of a massive oak known as the Council Oak. A meeting held beneath the oak in 1825 resulted in the treaty that opened the Santa Fe Trail.

I stopped in the Farmers & Drovers Bank to cash a traveler's check and asked Tim Garrett, a teller, about the park. "Half the people are for it and half against," he said. "Generally, the town people favor it, the ranchers are against it. They fear the government getting a foot in their door." I drove south on 177 through the gently undulating Flint Hills, a rich green in

the softly falling rain. In Strong City I talked with then Mayor Larry Bayer. "I think in two or three years we'll have a park here," he told me. The 10,894-acre Z-Bar Ranch on the north edge of town is being proposed as a Flint Hills Prairie National Monument. "It would certainly benefit the county," Larry said. "Like most small communities, we're dependent on agriculture, but it's just not working. In the last 15 years, Chase County has lost 15 percent of its population. Last year the Z-Bar was leased to a Texas firm. They trucked in Texas cattle in Texas trucks and had one overseer out there. In the fall, the Texas trucks came in, got the cattle, and took them away. There's no benefit to our area from that."

He envisions an increase in tourism for the area if the park becomes a reality. "We have people coming through here all the time who want to see prairie, to see what their ancestors went through. This would be the perfect place for them to see it."

The most peaceful place I saw with the word "prairie" attached was another cemetery, the Prairie Home Cemetery in Moorhead, Minnesota. It was a cold November morning, with squirrels making a racket in the dry leaves and a man walking his German shepherd. Traffic rumbled by. I wandered through, reading headstones. "Mother, rest in quiet sleep, while friends in sorrow o'er thee weep." Garrison Keillor got the name of his radio show—"A Prairie Home Companion"—from this cemetery. Identical

ANNIE GRIFFITHS BELT

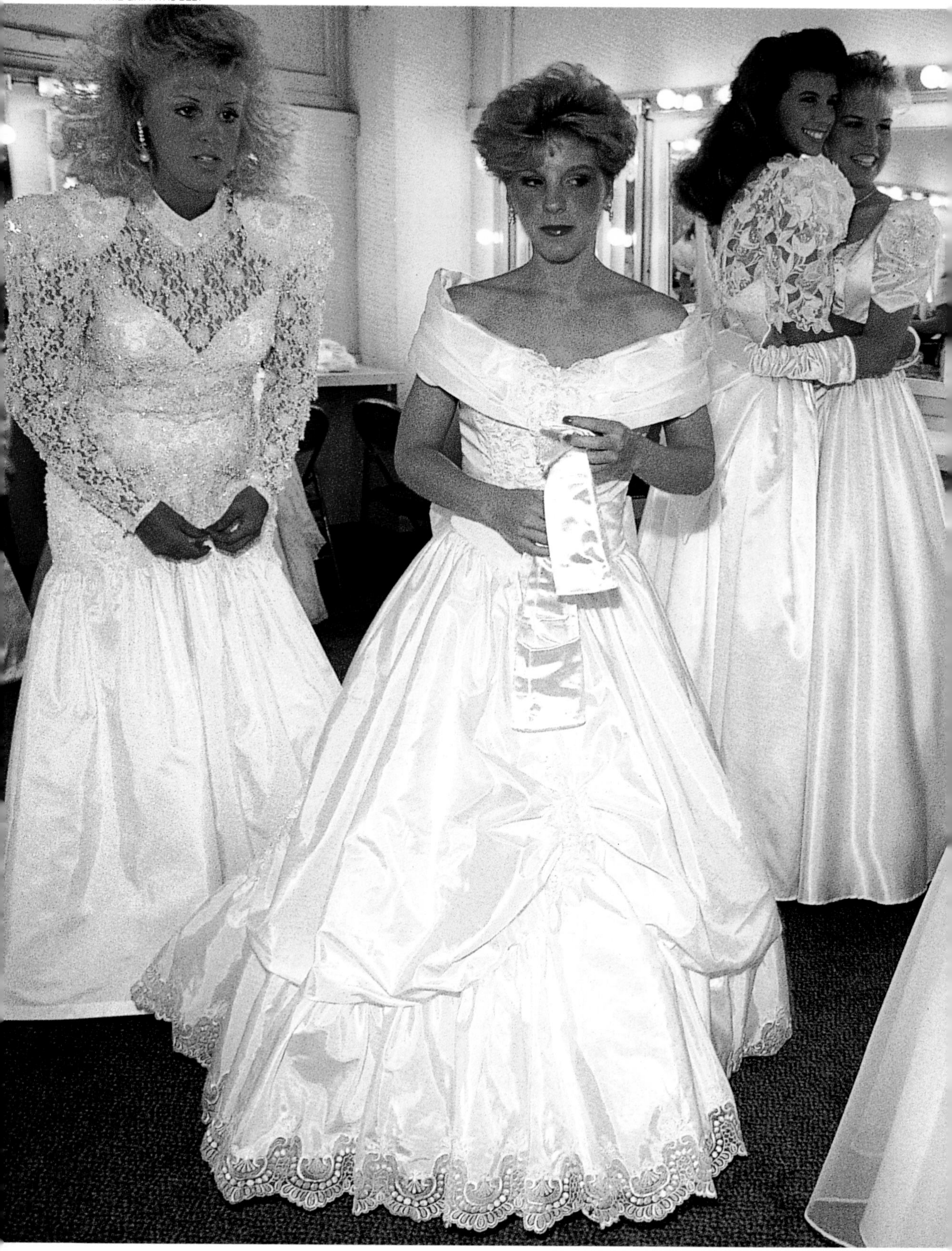

G*rown-up beauties in formal dresses pause before taking the stage for the 1990 Aquatennial coronation in Minneapolis, Minnesota. Winners of local glamour pageants held throughout the state meet in Minneapolis every summer and vie for the coveted title "Queen of the Lakes." Traci Erickson, Miss Columbia Heights (left), and Heather Scott, Miss Le Sueur (center), anxiously await the stage call. Sara Birkland, Miss Willmar Fest Queen, consults the mirror, while Joni Hathaway, Miss Isanti, trains her camera on two contestants hugging each other for good luck—Rebecca Hennessy, Miss Golden Valley (left), and Elisa Holton, Miss Richfield. Joni was named Miss Congeniality.*

Stranded motorist welcomes a tow truck near Fargo, North Dakota. The prairie lies open to howling winds and blowing snow. Drifts may erase all traces of roads, and the windchill can drop to levels as deadly as 100 degrees below zero.

headstones marked the graves of two sisters, Lillie G. and Jennie, who died on the same day, one 8, the other 13. "He shall gather the lambs into his arms and carry them into paradise."

Autumn in the prairies arrives early. By football season, you need a heavy jacket most places. And football season found me looking around for a game. I found two. In Maddock, North Dakota, I watched Maddock-Esmond play Sherwood in the opening round of the Class B 9-man high school football play-offs. In North Dakota, coach Dwight Leier told me, the 18 largest schools make up Class A. The next 36 in size are 11-man Class B teams. And all the rest—64 in the state—are 9-man Class B teams. "It makes for a more wide-open game with more scoring," he said. And he was right, as Maddock-Esmond put away Sherwood 43-6.

When I arrived, an hour before game time, Sherwood was on the field, warming up. There were bleachers only for the home-team fans; visitors stood. There were five tall poles on each side of the field, each with four lights. The Kallenbach brothers, Brad and Mikel, provided a good deal of the excitement for Maddock-Esmond. Each scored touchdowns, and each added extra points. It was odd to see a quarterback run for a touchdown, then change his shoe to kick the point after. *Lean to the left, lean to the right, stand up, sit down, fight, fight, fight!* A woman behind me in the stands had a voice like fingernails on a blackboard, and a little boy nearby was eating a hot dog that smelled so good I was tempted to take it away from him.

On another autumn day, I drove along Interstate 80 between the sprawls of Omaha and Lincoln, on my way to the Nebraska-Oklahoma State game, a long and serious rivalry in the Big Eight, the college conference that is most meaningful to heartland fans. Colorado, Iowa State, Kansas and Kansas State, Missouri, and Oklahoma complete the conference. Three of every four cars on the interstate carried people wearing red sweaters or red hats or red jackets—Nebraska fans. So I had no trouble finding the stadium.

In the press box high up on the side of the stadium, I had a pork sandwich and a soft drink, and watched the pregame activities. By 1:00 p.m. the stands were half full, and the teams were on the field doing calisthenics. They looked like dance groups. A U.S. flag soared aloft beneath a sleek kite. At 1:15 the Nebraska band came onto the field and formed a big N. Only the dull thump of the drums penetrated the press box. The band formed two lines for the team to run between as the sportswriters in the press box checked out the cheerleaders with their binoculars.

I could hear the roar of the crowd, a rising wave of sound, as the game began. The sky was a lumpy gray, and it looked chilly in the stands. Nebraska scored early, but only once in the half. At the end of each quarter, an assistant passed out mimeographed sheets of statistics.

Yellow penalty flags soar into the sky like rockets, as the crowd moans. A plane passes over, towing a banner: "Farmers and Ranchers for Ben Nelson." It's an election year. At halftime there are cookies and soft drinks in the press box while the band on the field goes silently through its numbers. The golden bells of the tubas sway in time to the music. A pigeon flies past my face. With the score 31-3, the crowd gets a wave going. With nine and a half minutes left to play, it begins to rain and people file for the exits. The score remains stuck at 31-3. The traffic jam on I-80 reaches to Omaha.

Geese, too, speak to me of autumn. As I sat waiting for a ferry to take me across the South Saskatchewan River north of Saskatoon, flocks were coming down the river, high up, heading south. In ragged V's they went over, flock after flock. It was like sitting at a busy airport and watching planes land. On the quiet ferry, I could hear their plaintive cries, high overhead. The elderly ferryman, who handled the big boat with delicacy, said softly, "Oh yes, the sky is full of birds."

In autumn, giant green corn pickers inch along two-lane blacktops or ply lush fields of ripe and rustling corn. About a fourth of all the cropland in the U.S. is planted in corn, sometimes called the "king of all farm crops." Near Volga, South Dakota, I drove west past fields of corn through patches of early morning fog that lay like thin, gauzy blankets over the farmland. Treetops protruded above them. Later in the morning, when it warmed up, I climbed up a five-rung ladder into a corn picker with Kent Howell, and we rode back and forth for a while together.

The cab, roomy and comfortable, was quiet enough for us to talk. Beneath our feet, stalks of corn disappeared hypnotically five rows at a time into the maw of the combine, which picks and shells the corn and flings the cobs aside. It took us about 10 minutes to make a trip the length of the field, 20 minutes round-trip. When our bin was full, we would stop and empty it into a wagon, which the hired man took back to the farm for drying.

"We're getting a good crop this year," Kent told me. "About 120 bushels an acre. Most of ours gets fed to our hogs, though this year we'll have some left over that we can sell." Kent sometimes spends 15 hours a day in the combine, and can harvest 5,000 bushels a day. He farms with his father and brother. "Grandfather started out in Iowa but lost everything in the Depression, so came up here in about 1940. I don't know if my children will be farmers. They've got the opportunity if they want to, I guess."

In the past, a young man could start a farm without a lot of capital. Farms were smaller then, and more self-sufficient, and a beginner could get a boost—perhaps some land and some used machinery—from his father. Now farms are bigger and machinery more sophisticated and expensive, and many farmers, encouraged to borrow heavily during the eighties, are barely afloat themselves. Few have the resources for helping a son start his own place.

"This combine would cost about $90,000 today," Kent said, "though they're like cars; you can get all kinds of extras on them. Not every farmer has one. We trade back and forth some. But when you need a combine, you need it now."

Halloween found me trick-or-treating with Debbie and Pete Isakson and their children Christopher, 5½, and Lea, 2½, in Devils Lake, North Dakota. It was a moonlit night, with a cool wind rustling the trees and the lawns piled with orange leaf bags imprinted with pumpkin faces. Chris was a clown; Lea, a pumpkin. We stopped at maybe 20 homes. It was easy to tell which were expecting us: open drapes, lots of lights on, pumpkins and decorations. Most of our victims were elderly. "Or what?" said one old-timer, to the traditional "Trick or treat!"

"His daughter used to baby-sit me," said Pete.

"We're making out like a bandit," said Chris. "It's going to be a feed."

Lea was a trooper. She walked with a purposeful stride, like someone on her way to work, and only complained when her sack began to get heavy. Several groups of children came and went on the dark street. At the front doors, they never learned to step back to let the storm doors open and risked being swept off the stoops.

Hannibal, Missouri—Mark Twain's hometown—had seemed an appropriate place to spend the Fourth of July. The town throws quite a celebration each summer, launching Tom Sawyer Days to coincide with the Fourth. Downtown Hannibal is turned over to a carnival, where toddlers shriek to be let off the miniature Ferris wheel, disappointing their macho fathers. Calliope music wafted through the air: "I've Got a Lovely Bunch of Cocoanuts."

I got my hair cut by a woman whose three-year-old son placed fourth in the Beautiful Baby Contest. He would have won, she believes, but the judge was a friend who "had to lean over backwards" to avoid favoring her.

Hannibal seemed as genteel as Aunt Polly herself, and Tom, I think, would feel right at home there. He and Becky are everywhere in evidence, but I didn't see much of Jim or Injun Joe or Huck or Huck's drunken Pap. Hannibal has chosen Tom as a suitably respectable symbol—mischievous, yes, but good-hearted and honest. You could describe the people of the prairie the same way.

It was hot in the afternoon when the parade came by. All the shady spots in the park were full, and the people at streetside used umbrellas as parasols. Congressman Harold Volkmer passed out fans that read "I'm a Fan of Congressman Volkmer." There were pretty girls in pretty cars, tap dancers, Civil War reenactors, Shriners. A radio station had its staff in the back of a pickup tossing ice cubes to the bystanders. The band *(Waiting on the levee, waiting for the Robert E. Lee. . . .)* was made up of costumed Toms and Beckys, the girls in gingham, the boys in ragged cutoff jeans.

Later I sat on a grassy bank near a marina to watch the fireworks. A family of ducks, undisturbed by people, was set into panicky, quacking flight by the fiery explosions overhead.

The expanding patterns rose over the broad Mississippi, trailing their gaudy reflections. The Mississippi gathers the waters of the heartland and sends them to the sea. From just downstream at St. Louis, Gateway to the West, the tributary Missouri reaches deep into the Great Plains states, its branches spreading all through them. The Mississippi is the river of the prairies, the Missouri the river of the plains.

Twain's Tom Sawyer seems like a prairie person, and he most likely hung around Hannibal. But Huck lit out for the territory. And so did I.

FOLLOWING PAGES: *Six starters, the entire offensive lineup, head for the gridiron in Chester, Nebraska. Six-man football, which originated in Chester in 1934, enables schools in sparsely populated towns to field a team. Fewer players fail to dull the fighting spirit of teams or fans. In a land often beset by extremes of nature, prairie dwellers hold to the belief that challenge builds character.*

The Plains

Where Buffalo Roamed

In the night, I wake to the sound of a lonely train whistle and realize with a start that it's my train. It's rolling across 800 miles of Canada, from Winnipeg to Edmonton, taking me from prairies to plains.

It is a sunny Monday afternoon, the first of October, when the train pulls out of Winnipeg, and the sun hurts my eyes as it glints off the golden stubble of the harvested wheat fields. Flocks of snow geese stand in the fields. Utility lines running alongside the train swoop up and down as we pass their poles. All the signs in the car are in both English and French: Fan—*Ventilateur*; Lights—*Eclairage*. There's a sudden clang of bells as we pass a crossing and sweep through a little town whose name I don't catch. It's funny to see Esso signs still in Canada. Suddenly we meet another train going the opposite direction, thundering by, four feet from my elbow. We cross a river and a fisherman looks up. Fields of sunflowers, corn, clumps of trees, scruffy little birches pass the window. Farmers are in their fields or bumping down dusty gravel roads in trucks full of hay bales.

Robert Louis Stevenson wrote, in *Across the Plains*, "It was a world almost without a feature; an empty sky, an empty earth; front and back, the line of the railroad stretched from horizon to horizon like a cue across a billiard-board."

In the dining car I talk with a Britisher on his way to visit his daughter in Australia and dine on something the menu calls chicken *grand-mère*, grandmother's chicken. We agree that there's nothing in the world any bleaker than a bleak little town far out on the plains, and discuss the fact that trains no longer go clickety-clack. After dinner it's dark outside, miles and miles of darkness: An occasional lonely pinpoint of light seems to say, Here we are. I get comfortable in my sleeper and settle down with Agatha Christie: "Miss Marple shook her head in a dissatisfied manner. 'I can't help feeling—I really can't—that it's not all quite as simple as that.'"

In the night, the silence of our stops awakens me, and the clatter of our movement lulls me back to sleep.

Perched just this side of nowhere, mechanic Robert Tanner tunes up an Aermotor in southeastern Colorado. Windmills made settlement possible in the plains.

PRECEDING PAGES: White and fluffy as a Saskatchewan snowstorm, an angora goat kid nuzzles Eve Beierbach on her family's ranch near Maple Creek.

It's cold and blustery in Edmonton in the morning. Gray clouds go scudding by overhead, and the wind hunches my shoulders and sends my cap flying. I rent a car and immediately get lost.

Edmonton, Canada's fifth largest city, takes me by surprise with its tangled web of streets spilling down the steep, wooded banks of the North Saskatchewan River. The first Edmonton, a fort built by the Hudson's Bay Company in 1795, was burned by Indians in 1807; the present city got a big surge of population in 1897–98 when thousands of gold seekers attempting the overland route to the Klondike gave up and settled here. The boom after World War II increased its population by 400 percent; today more than 600,000 people live here, and it's still growing.

Driving through Canada is only a little different from driving through the U.S., though everything seems bigger. It's been estimated that the eye takes in a hundred thousand acres at a glance here. Canada's Great Plains sweep northward from the border to the Arctic Circle. In an area not much larger than the Dakotas, the prairies of southern Alberta, Saskatchewan, and Manitoba represent 75 percent of Canada's farmland. As in the U.S., here lies the breadbasket. Southern Alberta produces a fourth of Canada's grain and beef, and in Saskatchewan the hardy descendants of early German, Ukrainian, and Scandinavian immigrants reap half of the country's wheat. This is especially significant because Canada produces far more of the grain than it consumes, ranking third (after the U.S. and France) among wheat-exporting nations—the world's emergency granary. And throughout, hundreds of oil wells rise amid the wheat fields.

As I drive, the radio sings American music: *I think you're out doin' what I'm home doin' without.* There are fewer fast-food places. Historical markers appear at roadside, but in Alberta there's no warning—you go sweeping right past them. The roadside symbol of Saskatchewan is a tiny shock of wheat, which looks like a fat mushroom. Roadside trash cans, a bright blue, are shaped like grain elevators. The people say "aboot" for about, and "oot" for out. There seem like a lot of dead coyotes alongside the road; I often see three or four in one day. In 1990 Saskatchewan is still suffering a paralyzing drought, and roadside potholes are dry and lake beds a dusty bluish-white. Wallace Stegner wrote of Saskatchewan: "Desolate? Forbidding? There was never a country that in its good moments was more beautiful. Even in drouth or dust storm or blizzard it is the reverse of monotonous, once you have submitted to it. . . ."

In Saskatoon during lunch I can hear six elderly ladies comparing tax stories. One, chagrined, says, "*Deborah* gets money back, *you* get money back, and I get bugger all." I'm in Saskatoon on Canada's Thanksgiving Day—October 8 this year—and spend it strolling along the Saskatchewan River with other park-goers. Magpies flutter overhead, and dry leaves crunch underfoot. I wander into the cool quiet of the Ukrainian Museum. Embroidered shirts and dresses, painted eggs, documents tracing the movement of the Ukrainians—the familiar story unfolds. Paintings honor the women; one shows a pioneer mother teaching her daughter to make the sign of the cross. Ukrainians also brought their knowledge of cold-weather wheat with them to Canada.

As in the prairies, I found that the Great Plains museums offered an introduction to an area. In summer they provided a cool respite from the ferocious heat and everlasting sunshine. I found, too, that there's a museum devoted to just about everything you can think of.

There's a National Wrestling Hall of Fame at Oklahoma State University in Stillwater that traces the sport back 5,000 years. The Petroleum Museum in Midland, Texas, has the "world's largest collection of antique drilling machinery and production equipment." In the Museum of the Plains Indian in Browning, Montana, there's a child's sled made of elk ribs and cowhide; its handle looks suspiciously like a cow's tail. A museum in Spearfish, South Dakota, was showing 72 portraits of Indians who fought at the Little Bighorn, painted in the 1930s and '40s. In the Stuhr Museum in Grand Island, Nebraska, I found a famous quote—"In God we trusted, in Nebraska we busted"—and a hard-to-believe fact: Two-thirds of Nebraska's prairie vegetation lies underground. Roots in a tangled mass, what we call sod, may reach six feet below the surface; they help prevent grasses from being permanently damaged by fire. There's a clipping from the Omaha *Daily Bee* of March 9, 1886: "Observers and scientific men agree that the turning up of the soil increased rainfall. . . ." The notion that rain followed the plow was the cruelest of the myths visited upon homesteaders in the Great Plains.

The museum in Jordan, Montana, had a model of a *Triceratops* skeleton found right there in Garfield County. The Pony Express Museum in Marysville, Kansas, displayed Indian artifacts and a huge collection of wrenches, painted different colors. There were photos on the wall: "Marysville's Only Hanging"—a corpse dangling from a bridge as young men lean over the railing for a closer look. And another photo: "Pony Express Rider Billy Richardson of St. Joseph, late in life." He still looked tough. The Cowboy Hall of Fame in Oklahoma City shows paintings by Russell, Remington, and Bierstadt, and a touching sculpture by James Earle Fraser, "The End of the Trail," a huge Indian slumped on a huge, exhausted horse.

The Pioneer Woman Museum in Ponca City, Oklahoma, had—my ideal—only one car in the parking lot. White-haired Roberta Newman was in charge. "I was born on 8th Street and live on 10th. In 70 years I've moved two blocks," she told me. "When we opened this place in 1957, I tried to get my mother to come down and see it. She said, 'I don't want to see all that old stuff. That's silly!' To us it's interesting and kind of romantic. To her it just represented hard work."

In Pine Bluffs, Wyoming, Barbara Zimmerman at the Texas Trail Museum of Laramie County was managing the perfect museum: *no* cars in the lot.

In fact, no lot, only a bare patch of earth alongside the street. Inside there was only the hum of light fixtures as I moseyed past fossils and arrowheads, homesteading artifacts, an old fire truck, and an even older switchboard.

Barbara put me in touch with Dr. Charles A. Reher, an archaeologist from the University of Wyoming who was born and reared in Pine Bluffs and who during recent summers has conducted a dig at the base of the bluffs. I sat with him atop them looking down on Interstate 80. "It's not for nothing that this area is called the Frontier Crossroads," he said. "Indians have been moving through here for 10,000 years. Frémont passed nearby in the 1840s. The Lodgepole Immigrant Trail, which connected with the Overland Trail in Laramie, was right over there. It was an alternate route during the Indian wars.

"Later, the Overland Stageline followed that creek you see across the highway north of Pine Bluffs. Over there, the Texas cattle trail came through in 1866, and the Union Pacific Railroad laid its tracks through Pine Bluffs in 1867. The Lincoln Highway, which became U.S. 30, arrived in 1913; now I-80 runs beside it. They put the transcontinental fiber optic cable through in the 1980s."

In northeast Wyoming, the Rockpile Museum in Gillette has one wall devoted to important women from the state's past: the first woman state superintendent of schools; the first woman mayor, elected in 1911; the first woman governor, Nelly Tayloe Ross, elected in 1924; and Mrs. Eliza A.

Swain, the first woman in the U.S. to vote in a general election, in 1920. "Mrs. Swain put on a clean white apron," reads the caption, "tied a shawl around her shoulders, and took a little tin pail with her; she had two errands to do; first, to take advantage of women's newly won privilege to vote, and second, to get a starter of yeast from a friend."

Frankie George was on duty the day I visited. She said, "The pioneer women were an independent, strong-willed lot. They worked as hard as the men, raising families and punching cows. And I expect they simply said, 'This is the way it's going to be.' I sometimes think we're more backward now than we were then."

The biggest-museum-in-the-smallest-town honors go to the Buffalo Trails Museum in Epping, North Dakota, population 104. Curator Elmer Halvorson retired from teaching art in the local high school in 1964 and has been working with the collection—which sprawls through seven buildings—ever since. "I was supposed to have help with the dioramas, but the guy died of a heart attack and that left them up to me, too," he told me. Elmer designed the layout and built the cases. He also constructed, out of papier-mâché, several life-size scenes, meticulously re-creating a period visit to the dentist, a courtship scene, a bedridden child. One of the buildings is a small log cabin. Inside hangs a photo of the woman who donated it to the museum. Elmer said: "Her husband came back to their sod home one day with a load of logs, and she said, 'Andrew, what are you doing?' And he said, 'Sophie, I'm going to build a barn for the cow.' 'Oh no you're not,' she said. 'Andrew, you're going to build me a house.' And this is it."

Unlike most of the museums in the plains, the Oklahoma City Art Museum hangs no paintings of buffalo hunts or cowboys. Instead there's a room full of Andy Warhol soup cans, along with a varied collection that includes Thomas Hart Benton, Roy Lichtenstein, Picasso, Gauguin, and Louise Nevelson. The mansion that holds the collection was once the home of Frank Buttram, a geologist in the early days of the oil industry in Oklahoma. His tastes ran more to his collection of 52 old masters, his son Dorsey told me, acquired in the '20s and '30s during extensive travels throughout the world. He was active in city, state, and national affairs but was proud, too, said Dorsey, of striking out Ty Cobb three times while in college.

"They finished building the house in 1938, when I was away at school," Dorsey told me. "Then the war came, and after that, work took me away

Six-year-old Tina Kelly and teacher Kendra Jammerman ponder time's mysteries in a one-room schoolhouse on the Vinton ranch near Gordon, Nebraska.

PRECEDING PAGES: Mrs. Jammerman and all her pupils gather for the daily pledge of allegiance. Horses serve as transportation to school.

from home. So, though I watched the house being built, I didn't get to live in it as much as I'd have liked."

Active patrons of the arts, Dorsey and his wife, Phyllis, sponsor an annual competition among high school string musicians. "This was always a musical home," Dorsey told me. "Mother would sometimes have as many as 200 people in for a musical evening. She said one time, 'If we don't encourage young local performers, we won't have a symphony in the future. There won't be anyone to replace the musicians.' " Phyllis is active in fund-raising for the arts. "It was easier in the late '70s and early '80s," she told me, "when there was new money around. One year we raised $700,000 and got the symphony completely out of debt. There were a lot of young oilies wanting to be plucked, and we plucked 'em."

Each year the winners of the high school competition present a recital in the museum, and I happened to be in town for 1990's. Saint-Saëns, Handel, Mozart—the music filled the spacious, elegant rooms. Erica Wolfe, a very poised high school sophomore from Tulsa, won the award as best violin soloist, and played a sprightly movement of a Mozart concerto and a tricky Bartók dance.

The oil and gas industry that Dorsey's father helped to found is much in evidence in this part of the plains. Often as I drove through Texas and Oklahoma, I'd get a whiff of the oil fields; it's as if a stove's pilot light had gone out. Nodding donkeys nod in pastures and backyards, and the orange flare of burning waste gas can often be seen in the distance.

Near Elk City, in western Oklahoma, Merle Blau showed me around Parker Drilling Company's rig 201, which will one day be one of the world's deepest gas wells. They were down to 18,227 feet when I was there, and, at 3 feet per hour, they were headed for 28,800. The giant rig groaned and shrieked as the drill inched deeper into the ground. The bit is made of tungsten and costs $30,000; one can last about 200 hours, depending on what it's drilling through. "People back East complain about how much gas costs, but it costs a lot to get it out of the ground, too," said Merle. The rig cost 12 million dollars in 1974 but is expected to pay for itself in three years, after it starts producing gas. We stopped by the geologist's shed, where detailed seismic portraits of nearby wells, tacked to the wall alongside a portrait of this one, tell drillers what they can expect to encounter next. It's like comparing tree rings. A 12-foot-by-22-foot American flag flew atop the rig.

Rig 201 was larger by far than an entire town I found one pleasant day in eastern Montana. I had lunched at the Montanan Café in Broadus—egg salad sandwich, potato soup, iced tea, coffee, and a chocolate cream pie that nearly made me cry, for $5.35—and was heading north alongside the Powder River. This is the sandy, turquoise green river that cowboys said was a mile wide and an inch deep. Braids and sandbars confused its currents, and cottonwoods dotted its banks. Magpies flitted among the branches. Prong-horns watched me pass. Their eyesight has been compared to that of a human using 8-power binoculars. A fox looked over its shoulder at me, and a big mule deer stood in the middle of the road. Sheep shared the right-of-way, along with wild turkeys and cottontails. Rugged hills and scraggly trees and sagebrush, mile after mile after mile—this is some of the loneliest country in the lower 48 states. A bicycle leaned against a mailbox at the end of a driveway that was easily a mile long. Two ranchers on mopeds were moving cattle in a field across the river.

Suddenly on my right was a small wood-frame building with jungle gyms and swings, and a flag flying out front—the Powderville School, I found, when I inquired the next day. Inside were Mrs. Joanie Reed and her five students, one each in the third, fourth, fifth, sixth, and eighth grades: Missy, James, David, Kimberly, and Kimberly's brother J. J.

Their schoolroom was square, with large windows on two sides and a green blackboard up front. Bookshelves, maps, pictures, posters, and Halloween art covered the walls. There was a large air-conditioning unit in one window, a computer and a VCR in one corner.

It's been said that students in a one-room schoolhouse learn three ways: They overhear students ahead of them doing lessons, they do the lessons, and they have the lessons reinforced by overhearing students coming along behind them. Montana has more than a hundred such schoolhouses, yet consistently ranks in the upper 10 percent in student achievement tests.

I sit for a couple of hours with Mrs. Reed and the children. James, who was absent yesterday, is doing yesterday's math. Missy has a question about carrying. J. J. has a math problem whose answer is 3.6 x 104. Mrs. Reed strolls from place to place, looking over shoulders. "You have a very neat paper, Kim." James yawns and looks out the window. He's wearing red-and-black cowboy boots. David, doing a story problem, has a question: "But he got two pounds of beef, right?" It's time to switch to English lessons, and James and David groan and try to get the assignment reduced. Missy says, "I've got 53 problems, and I'm only on 19." Mrs. Reed sits at her desk and corrects math papers while they work. They're adorable when they concentrate. They're all wearing jeans and T-shirts except Missy, who has on a sweater. She says, "I'll probably have to take my math home." Mrs. Reed says, "Don't spend so much time counting up how many you have left." J. J. yawns and looks at the clock. "Seven minutes!" James finishes his math and asks, "Can I read now?" Missy toys with her hair. She has pink shoe laces in her sneakers. James begins reading *Riding the Pony Express.* Mrs. Reed walks past his desk *(Continued on page 118)*

FOLLOWING PAGES: *Premier threat of the plains, a funnel cloud reels unpredictably across a West Texas skyline spewing earthly debris. Clashes between warm, moist air from the Gulf and dry, northern blasts spawn some 850 twisters yearly in the U.S., many in a Texas-to-Nebraska belt renowned as Tornado Alley.*

*F*lash of hands and cards—
and sometimes a winner's smile—
brighten the green baize of Saloon
No. 10 in Deadwood, South
Dakota, as a poker-faced dealer plies
her trade. One of several gambling
halls in this Black Hills town, No. 10
takes its name from the Deadwood
bar where Wild Bill Hickok lost his
life in 1876, holding what became
known as the "dead man's hand"—
aces over eights. Deadwood
boomed during the Black Hills gold
rush of the 1870s; then fire, flood,
Prohibition, and—worst of all—a
1964 ban on gambling brought the
town to the brink of economic ruin.
Gambling's 1989 re-legalization
has sparked a return of boom times,
based less on mining and more on
tourists eager for a wilder West.

and picks up a couple of pencils from the floor. "Thank you," he whispers.

"The girls usually finish before the boys," David confides to me. He has three sisters, all of whom attended Powderville School. Two are in college now, one goes to high school in Broadus. J. J. is working on possessives (goose's, geese's) and plurals (leaf, leaves). David is at the computer, doing a geography lesson. James says his grandmother told him locusts do no damage. "Let's look it up in the encyclopedia after lunch," says Mrs. Reed. At recess she tells me a story about James. "A while back he had the word 'forbid' in a vocabulary lesson and wanted to know what it meant. I said, 'Well, your mother might forbid you to get out your dad's guns to look at when she's not home.' He said, 'She doesn't let me go up to the house when she's not there. She says it's against the law.' "

Mrs. Reed prepares lessons in four or five different subjects, every night, for five grades, even though there's only one student in each grade, so she is by far the hardest worker in the school.

"What do students miss out on, going here?" I asked her. "Well," she said, "when there's only one student in a class, they don't have any competition. And we can't offer physical education, there's no gym, no team sports. But generally, though we're not immune from the big-city schools' problems of drugs and violence, we're less apt to have them."

Garfield County's high school students are similarly remote. Jordan is the most isolated county seat in the lower 48 and site of the county's only high school. With just 1,600 people to tax, Garfield County is sometimes hard-pressed to maintain its roads and bridges, public services, and schools. The tax base is just five million dollars, and the total income from taxes in a year is just one and a half million dollars. Any emergency expense that comes up has to be met with a special assessment.

High school students come from all over its 5,000 square miles, and for many—especially those involved in after-school activities or those at the end of the 30- to 40-mile bus routes—it's not easy to get home again. So Jordan provides an in-town dormitory, funded partly by the parents and partly by the county and the state. There were once a number of such dorms in Montana, but Jordan's is the only one still in operation.

I stopped by and talked with Mrs. Claudia Stanton, in her sixth year as dorm matron, whose job is to keep order and provide the students with two meals a day, breakfast and dinner. "I've got twenty-five this year," she told me. "Ten girls and fifteen boys." She showed me through the dorm, a large,

Grain elevator manager Larry Seaman of Hubbell, Nebraska, wades into a two-story-high mound of milo, or grain sorghum, left unsheltered by elevators already full to bursting. Milo—southern Nebraska's primary summer crop—mainly feeds cattle; it sheds water readily and weathers outdoor storage well.

three-story frame building. The kitchen, the dining area, the rec room "where they tear things up. Boys cannot sit down gently on a sofa.

"They have their supper at 6:00, or whenever they finish their after-school activities. Then they have clean-up duties in their rooms or help with the common areas. At 6:45 they're free to go out, but they have to be back in at 9:00. From 9:15 to 10:00 is study time, then lights out. They can have radios as long as they're at a dull roar. If you've got rock 'n' roll at this end of the hall and country-western at that end. . . ." Most go home for weekends, but some stay, especially if there's a Friday night football game.

"This is the girls' floor," said Claudia, as we climbed another flight of stairs. "I try to keep them separate, though one year I had a boy who thought he was God's gift to womanhood." Claudia buys the food, plans the menus, does the cooking. "They'd love it if I served nothing but pizza, hamburgers, spaghetti, and tacos. If I fix a nice roast, they'll say, 'Yuck, we have that at home.'"

It's sometimes hard on the youngsters, being away from home at age 13

or 14. "Oh, I've sat with one a time or two. You can tell they're having trouble. One said to me one time, 'You don't know what it feels like to be dropped at that front door and have your folks drive away.' "

Generally they're well behaved. "I like the sports for that reason," said Claudia. "It tires them out. The boys were so tired last night I didn't have to say anything to them about bedtime. The coach had got disgusted with them and made them run laps. They were dragging when they came in. Did their homework and were ready for bed."

I met more high school students in Oklahoma, a thousand miles southeast across the plains. A newspaper story named the state's high school Future Farmers of America Star Agri-Businessman of the Year and Star Farmer of the Year.

Howard Kohn, in *The Last Farmer*, remembers the FFA of his youth as "farming for ribbons." He writes, "There are some boys, gifted with discipline, authoritatively gung ho, who have the aura of the land, and who do things—get up before dawn, read the latest literature, become impatient for the first thaw, talk crop yields to their dates—that mark them indelibly as future farmers." I found Brandon Yost and Bartt Smith not quite to fit the mold, though certainly serious and levelheaded. (And girls, having broken the mold altogether, now make up 30 percent of FFA membership.)

The wind was rippling the wheat the day I looked up Brandon. The landscape of the plains is often accused of being boring. A specific scene may be full of detail: rolling hills and nodding, rust-colored grasses, an occasional slough or ravine, once in a while a clump of wind-bent trees. The problem is: It goes on and on and on. It's endlessly repeated for hundreds of miles in every direction. The landscape itself isn't boring, there's just too much of it.

Star Farmer of the Year, Brandon lives near Kingfisher and goes to a high school with 435 students. I drove with him and his FFA adviser for a while through the countryside. On a golf course, two women were peering intently down into the shallows of a water hazard. Oops. *I've never lost at love, not counting you,* sang the radio. At 18, Brandon operates three farms. He's been given a good start by his grandfather and father, who have farmed successfully in the area for many years. Though Kingfisher calls itself the Buckle on the Wheat Belt, Brandon's specialty is cattle. He buys calves, fattens them up for six months or so, then sells them to feedlots in Kansas or to operations like the Veatches' in Illinois.

"As Grandfather gets older, he's farming less," Brandon told me. "He

just has about 400 acres now, enough to kind of piddle with. This is one of my farms over here. It'll be harvested just for the grain."

Brandon made it all sound pretty easy. "What can go wrong with a cattle operation?" I asked him.

"Well, they can all die."

He planned to attend Oklahoma State University in Stillwater in the fall, to major in animal sciences and agronomy. "What would you want to do if for some reason you couldn't farm?" I asked him, and he thought and thought but couldn't come up with anything. I slipped him a pop quiz. "I've been trying to remember," I said, "the words to that song about Oklahoma. Something about wind and wheat." Without stopping to think, he said, "The waving wheat can sure smell sweet when the wind comes right behind the rain."

Bartt Smith, Star Agri-Businessman, lives in Laverne at the eastern edge of the Oklahoma Panhandle. There 54 students take part in FFA, a third of the student body. Bartt earned money while in high school by harvesting other people's wheat. He too is going to OSU, to major in Ag Ed. He wants to teach. He built a two-wheel trailer that picks up the big, round bales of hay that weigh between 1,200 and 2,000 *(Continued on page 126)*

*H*omegrown talent packs the courthouse lawn
as first-graders perform the "Ballet of the Enchanted Dolls"
in Phillipsburg, Kansas, during its annual Riverless
Festival—a play on nearby Wichita's Riverfest.
Phillipsburg High School juniors John Staab and Stacy
Moffat (above) lead the commencement march.

FOLLOWING PAGES: Largest coal mine in the U.S.,
Wyoming's Black Thunder operation annually strips
30 million tons of raw energy from an immense bed near
Wright. Low price and low sulfur content help make
this bonanza competitive with eastern mines.

pounds. These are the ones that, set in a row, look like giant Tootsie Rolls.

Bartt, too, failed to come up with another career he'd choose if he couldn't farm. "If I'm not working, I'm doing sports," he said. "I got second in the state in the high jump last year, and hope to get first this year." Sure enough, the following weekend at the state finals in Yukon, I watched as Bartt cleared six feet, two inches in the high jump, and won first place.

Earth Day found me still in Oklahoma, so I dropped by the Tulsa Zoo, where festivities were planned. Tulsa was once called Tulsey Town and grew from a post office established in 1879. Today its fortunes rise and fall with the oil industry.

At the zoo, toddlers in their strollers were turning pink in the broiling sun even before they got inside the zoo. A bridge from the parking lot to the zoo crossed a muddy stream, where turtles lazily swam. A little girl looking down on them cried, "Mommy, look! Nature!"

Polar bears splashing in ice blue water looked coolest. Large wooden umbrellas 20 feet high offered shade to the giraffes. Lions dozed on their sides. Squirrels, not part of the official zoo population, sniffed in the grass, and monkeys lazed in leafy shade high in their trees. Booths set up by environmental organizations lined the walks. Near me a mother felt her baby's behind. "I bet you need a change. This is the problem with using environmentally sound diapers. But, I figure if my mom could do it with five kids. . . ." I bought a T-shirt from Friends of the Earth and collected pamphlets from the Sierra Club, the Oklahoma Wildlife Federation, the Lung Association of Tulsa County, the Tulsa Audubon Society. In the Audubon handout I read, "An unusual report by Bob Jennings is of a Prairie Chicken that flew into the window of Boston Avenue Methodist Church at 13th St. & Boston breaking the window as well as its neck." A handout from the Tulsa S.P.C.A. declared, "We speak for those who cannot speak for themselves."

Three states north in South Dakota, Dayton Hyde speaks loudly for those who can't speak for themselves. He has established a nonprofit, 50,000-acre sanctuary for wild mustangs, some of it in the ruggedly beautiful grasslands of the Black Hills and the rest along Little White River. Mustangs, notoriously tough and energetic, are descended from horses brought to the New World by Spanish explorers and settlers. Since 1971 it has been the policy of the Bureau of Land Management (BLM) to round up those wild horses in the West that exceed the carrying capacity of the public range. They are put up for adoption, and more than 70 percent find a home. But many are too old, too unattractive, or too sickly to be adopted, and are condemned to living out their lives miserably in crowded pens. It is to them that Dayton's heart goes out.

With the cooperation of the BLM, he trucks these rejects to his sanctuaries in South Dakota and turns them loose on large, fenced, private-land ranges. No stallions allowed, only geldings and mares, so there's no danger that the horses will breed and overwhelm their range.

We put a couple of sacks of grain in the back of Dayton's pickup and drove out among them. Small herds pricked up their ears and watched us with interest. We stopped, and Dayton put a few handfuls of grain out on the ground. The horses ambled up, shouldering one another aside, watching us carefully but obviously at ease. They may have been the rejects, but they looked handsome and healthy.

"Back in 1939 I came upon nearly 40 horses that had starved to death," Dayton told me. "It was a haunting sight, a sight I'll never forget. For years, you could ride back there and see the effect they had had on the trees and bushes before they died. I guess that gave me a special feeling for horses that are in trouble.

"I like being around these animals, whether I ride them or not. They're friends. Sometimes I just come out here and sit with them.

"When we bring them in in the trucks, we turn them out first into corrals, then open the gates. They stand around for a few minutes until they realize they're free. Then, I wish you could see them, the joy and the exuberance. . . ."

Horses came walking toward us, down out of clumps of trees, off

"It's Stonehenge for America," jokes owner Stanley Marsh 3 of ten half-buried cars arrayed on his spread west of Amarillo, Texas. Pop artists, known as "Ant Farm," created this sculpture in 1974 and dubbed it "Cadillac Ranch."

JOEL SARTORE

ridges, a pretty sight. "There's my girlfriend," said Dayton. "She and another were near death—malnourished, weak, skin and bones. They could hardly stand. They didn't care if they lived or died. I packed water out here to them because they couldn't get to their feet. They remember."

Their troubles seemed to be over but aren't. I left Dayton worrying about how to raise three million dollars to pay for the land he's using as sanctuaries.

A woman farther south, in Denton, Texas, devotes her efforts to the plants rather than the animals of the Great Plains. Barbara Lea Anthony, the Wildflower Lady of North Texas according to the local newspaper, devises ways to make seeds grow. The Texas Seed Collectors Association gathers seeds of wildflowers from the Texas plains and sends them to Barbara, who propagates them—not always an easy proposition.

Denton is northwest of and not far from Dallas, out where the West begins. About here, "the land grows rougher, the trees thinner, the cowboys' drawl more pronounced," according to Ed Syers in *Backroads of Texas*.

With peacocks screaming in the background, I walked with Barbara through her greenhouse, a bright, humid building full of flats of sprouts and seedlings. Her hobby has grown into a full-time passion. Mexican hat, baptisia, Indian blankets, bluebonnets, bluebells, evening primroses, winecups, bee balm, horsemint—their names were as varied as their separate problems. "This one I froze, boiled, soaked, and then planted. It made me so mad." To support her hobby, Barbara sells ordinary plants—even geraniums—and vegetables at the local farmers' market. "This is a fairly new science," she told me. "We're not trying to hybridize, not trying to cross them; we're just trying to see what mother nature does to make them grow." She even soaks some stubborn seeds in ethylene gas. "It's fairly natural, when you think about it," she said. "If you cut an apple in half and put it in a plastic bag, you produce ethylene. It's a natural substance. My hunch is, perhaps some plants have adapted to growing beneath fruit trees, where they might receive a signal to grow from the juices of rotting fruit."

When Barbara is successful, she presents the plants to the Thomsen Foundation, an organization supporting prairie restoration; several hundred acres of land in nearby Montague County are becoming a showcase of Great Plains wildflowers.

I spend a lot of time driving through the Great Plains states. In Kansas, wind hits the car with a sudden slap. UPS trucks are everywhere. Black, barrel-shaped clouds tumble over one another, and the sky takes on an Old Testament look. Sitting in my car one day waiting out a rainstorm, I feel the thunder physically shake the car. Here men wear belts with their name across the back—"Johnny"—and buckles the size of saucers. *It may be the truth, or it may be a lie, but it sounds like the sound of good-bye,* the radio sings. West of Salina, the smell of freshly mown hay comes in the car window and sits me up straight. In Dodge City, I stop by a Babe Ruth League game on a benign summer evening. A beetle high in the lights falls to the bleachers beside me, lands on its back, wiggles its legs. Three of the first five batters are named Jason. Heading toward Garden City, there's a sudden flurry of animals. I barely miss a snake sidewinding its way across the road, then there's a thump as a red-winged blackbird hits the corner of the windshield, then the car immediately straddles a tiny turtle. In the mirror I see it has come to a stop and is tucking itself in. Two crows sitting on adjacent fence posts turn and glare at each other.

Kansas probably has been the butt of more sarcasm and jokes than any other state. A professor at Kansas University once said of Kansas, "You can look farther and see less than any place in the world except Texas." Sinclair Lewis's fictional Kansan, Elmer Gantry, spoke of his hometown of "plodding yokels." Kansas was first with Prohibition and home to Carry Nation. But then Superman grew up in Kansas, too. Riding up Pikes Peak, I shared a seat with a middle-aged couple from Topeka. When I praised their capitol building, they blushed and squirmed with pleasure. Kansans aren't used to compliments.

One gusty Sunday I head west from Grand Island, Nebraska, on the Lincoln Highway, U.S. 30. Small, brown corn husks skitter across the road, and tumbleweed piles up against fences like animals trying to get over. I come across white wooden churches with half a dozen cars parked in front. Songbirds lift up out of roadside weeds and are wafted away on the wind. A train full of coal clatters eastward. It's raining hard now, but Lexington has its water sprinkler running in a little triangular park by the highway. The post office in Willow Island is a mobile home with a flag out front. About two minutes after leaving one little town, I see the grain elevators of the next one. The brightest items in some of the towns are the new stars at the Texaco stations; the most faded, the stop signs. I meet another coal train, and another. Where is all this coal coming from? *I'm the train they call the City of New Orleans,* comes from the radio, just as I'm passed by a Union Pacific train. A woman giving the market report from Omaha says, "Everything's up in beans"; farmers in the heartland succeed or fail on just such announcements. There's a big John Deere dealership at the edge of a town; gangly green-and-yellow machines look like somebody's collection of insects pinned to a board, all the beetles over here, all the grasshoppers over there. In the national grasslands, missile silos appear to be the dominant works of man. There's a meadowlark on every third telephone pole, and little gravel roads run at perfect right angles past an occasional abandoned house. I pass a feedlot full of cattle, and *(Continued on page 136)*

FOLLOWING PAGES: Overseeing a part of his checkerboard empire, Paul Engler surveys a feedlot near Cactus, Texas, one of five he owns. The self-styled "world's largest custom cattle feeder" says his yards fatten some 800,000 head a year.

*S*porting a mustache no
Marlboro man could rival, cowboy
Rod Smith relaxes between roundup
chores at the 39,000-acre Cross H
Ranch near Post, Texas. The town of
4,000 residents takes its name from
founder Charles William Post, the
cereal magnate of Postum and Post
Toasties fame. In 1907, he began
developing some 330 square miles
of plains land into a "farm colony,"
a planned community of satellite
farms and ranches surrounding a
central town. Post had complete
farms built—including wells,
outbuildings, fences, and other
necessities—then sold them to
settlers on installment. Cotton
became both the main agricultural
product and the local industry, as
Post installed textile mills that
ensured an integrated cottonfield-
to-pillowcase operation.

*C*ultural crossroads in the heart of cattle country, the West Texas town of
Post stages *Romeo and Juliet* beneath a haloed buffalo skull. A few blocks away,
Lou Ann Ammons celebrates her quinceañera—*fifteenth birthday*—flanked by
her "court" of damitas—*little ladies*. The party, inspired by a Mexican rite of
passage, throbs to mariachi music. Rich or poor, the host family traditionally
spends lavishly on this fiesta, whose importance in a young girl's life is second
only to her wedding. Such celebrations help realize the vision of founder C. W.
Post: a dream city complete with tree-shaded streets and varied culture.

the smell stays with me for 2.6 miles. A cloud of fragrant white smoke rises on the left: farmers burning a pasture. At Wildcat Hills State Recreation Area, a sign reads, "Caution. Rattlesnakes In This Area," and on the path someone has painted "Trust Jesus." I do, but I watch my step just the same. I stop at a marker that tells of an Indian attack on a train. "At dawn the Indians rode away with bolts of bright colored calico tied to their ponies' tails."

Pat and Wendy Vinton ranch in western Nebraska's desolate Sand Hills, the largest tract of mixed and tallgrass prairie remaining in North America. The Plains Indians hunted buffalo here until after the Civil War. The Sand Hills became cattle ranching country in the 1870s and '80s. Grass-covered dunes occupy some 19,000 square miles. Windmills whirl like crazy, pumping up little dribbles of water that are immediately turned to mist by the wind. Plants have adapted to survive in the shifting sand. Some put down deep taproots; others spread extensive root systems near the surface, which helps them capture water and also binds the loose soil. A bush morning glory's roots may descend 10 feet and fan out 15 to 25 feet in all directions. Lakes occur where depressions are lower than the water table.

The Vintons maintain something between 100 and 140 miles of fence, and all their animals are friendly. My guide on the ranch was 8-year-old Merici. She put me aboard Benji and off we went to help her father and several hands move some cattle. Benji was my kind of horse: Nothing would induce him to go faster than a slow walk. Occasionally we would lose sight of the other riders. Benji would stop in his tracks, prick up his ears, and scan the horizon until he spotted another rider. Then off we would plod in *that* direction. The hands were Jay, a large, quiet cowboy; Richard, from Ireland, who was spending three months in the States; and Willy, from Gillette, Wyoming. I asked Richard what he missed from Ireland. "Scenery," he laughed. When Willy learned I was headed for Gillette, he gave me a tip. "Check out the coal. Coal is the most important thing in that part of Wyoming." So *that's* where all that coal was coming from.

Concerning the coal mines of eastern Wyoming, David Costello wrote, "Here, radiant energy stored in the Paleozoic swamps more than 300 million years ago is being converted into modern electrical energy. The thought occurs to you that this place was not always prairie."

Willy even gave me the name of a mine, probably the best name for a coal mine ever devised: Black Thunder, an operation of the Thunder Basin Coal Company.

In terms of the amount of coal produced in a year—30 million tons—Black Thunder is the largest coal mine in the U.S. It and a dozen others are in Campbell County, and if Campbell County were a country, its coal reserves would be among the ten largest in the world. And if the Black Thunder mine were a state, it would rank 11th in the U.S. in coal production.

Jim Herickhoff, the president, and Jim Comer, production manager, put me into a yellow hard hat and a van and showed me around. "The Powder River Basin is an enormous syncline," Herickhoff told me, "shaped like a bowl. There's a huge bed of coal forming it. It reaches the surface here in eastern Wyoming and up around Coalstrip, Montana. We're in effect mining the edges of the bowl, where they reach the surface, but there are billions of tons more coal inside the edges."

Black Thunder is a big hole in the ground that moves. As overburden is removed on one edge of the hole, reclamation is proceeding to the rear. The miners are justly proud of their reclamation efforts. "Since 1978 we've spent more than 35 million dollars for dust control, reclamation, revegetation, waste processing, and for studies of the vegetation, soils, geology, wildlife, water, climate, land use, and archaeology of our site," Herickhoff said. They plant 21 species of forbs, grasses, and shrubs on freshly placed topsoil when they're finished with an area. Cattle and pronghorns routinely graze reclaimed areas, and a herd of elk had recently moved into another one. I couldn't distinguish areas that had been mined from areas that had not, although I expect a specialist could. It should be noted that county, state, and federal regulations require this reclamation.

"When they talk about clean western coal, this is what they're talking about," said Comer. The seam of coal is 70 feet thick.

Everything at Black Thunder is bigger than anywhere else. Trucks that haul the coal from the seam up to the crushers hold 240 tons—two and a half railroad cars full. They have 2,200-horsepower engines, and the operator sits in a cab 23 feet above the ground. They have "King of the Lode" painted across their fronts. The tires weigh 8,000 pounds each and are 11 feet tall. "One truckload of coal would heat an average home for 40 years," said Herickhoff.

Thor, the dragline that removes the overburden, takes 90 cubic yards with one bite. It weighs 7.2 million pounds. We watched it move back a few feet. Ponderous and massive, it nonetheless moved fairly gracefully. Two tiny men walked alongside it, communicating with the operator by radio. Delicate puffs of dust rose at each step.

One ton of Thunder Basin coal equals approximately three barrels of oil; thus Thunder Basin mines the Btu equivalent of 270,000 barrels of oil each day. "As long as it's the truth, it ain't braggin'," said Herickhoff.

In the plains of Texas I see trains of tank cars instead of coal. "Don't Mess With Texas," say the signs, and "Drive Friendly." A radio station boasts, "The Big Country's best country is Wizard 103.7 in Abilene." *There's a chalk silhouette on the floor where they found me alone in the dark; medical examiner said, 'This boy*

FOLLOWING PAGES: Like a mirage out of Eastern Europe, an onion-domed Ukrainian Catholic church rises unexpectedly from the plains of Model Farm township, Saskatchewan. The structure recalls the ethnic roots of 19th-century pioneers, whose descendants reenact the traditional Good Friday procession.

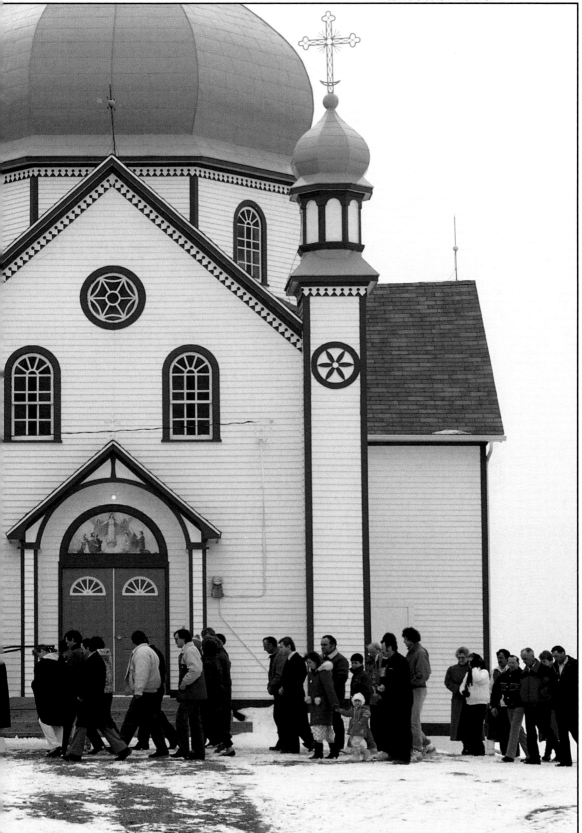

Entire senior class of Bethune, Colorado, lines up outside school on the state's high eastern plains, where large farms and feedlots predominate. Limited opportunity and the lure of city lights draw youth from small plains towns like Bethune, sapping rural population. Not leaving, just moving on: Tumbleweed (opposite) skitters down a desolate eastern Colorado highway, propelled by fierce wind and a mixture of snow and dirt, known to locals as "snirt."

died of a broken heart.' Walter Prescott Webb wrote of Abilene: "On the surface Abilene was corruption personified. Life was hectic, raw, lurid, awful." We're a long way from *Little House on the Prairie*.

In Muleshoe there's a statue of a mule: "without ancestral pride or hope for offspring. . . ." I drive from Dallas to Paris along roadsides lush with bluebells. "Welcome to Honey Grove, Sweetest Town in Texas." In the Dairy Queen there I hear a man say, "The only good wax is a buff wax." At the Eagles Nest Café in Goldthwaite I'm eating a piece of chocolate cream pie when three tough-looking cowboys come in and walk past me to a table. I hear one whisper to his companions, with barely contained anticipation: *"Chocolate pie!"* Cowboys leave their hats on when they eat, and the old-timers rock from side to side when they walk. I see a newspaper ad for a hat store: "Cowboys Don't Carry Umbrellas."

A sign in front of the American Cotton Growers in Littlefield proclaims

the town "Denim Capital of the West." Denim is now the ubiquitous fabric of the world, but it takes its character from the American West.

"We're a farmer-owned cooperative set up to produce denim," personnel director Danny Davis told me, when I visited the plant just off Waylon Jennings Boulevard. "The vast majority of our denim is sold to Levi Strauss. If you buy a pair of Levi's of heavy-weight denim, there's a pretty good chance the fabric came from here." The firm weaves 80,000 linear yards of denim a day, or 28 million yards a year. That's enough to make something over 20 million pairs of jeans. The plant—10 acres under one roof; 500 employees—was a-clatter with complex machinery doing intricate things at lightning speed. Robots prowled a spinning machine, looking for broken threads. Nearly 400 looms, in row after row, shuddered and rattled as they laced warp (lengthwise indigo yarn) and filling (natural-colored crosswise yarn) into 100 percent cotton denim. *(Continued on page 146)*

*R*anching's lonely labors: A hired hand chops ice from a stock pond on the Bledsoe Ranch in eastern Colorado. As much as anything on the plains, spring means calving season; a newborn might need help in climbing to its feet.

FOLLOWING PAGES: Like cowhands responding to a dinner bell—only slower—cattle amble toward a just-arrived pickup load of hay. Says Chris Bledsoe, co-owner of the 12,000-acre spread, "You can't believe the blizzards here. With 50-, 80-, 100-mile-per-hour winds, it's a total whiteout for two, three days at a time."

Airborne medic for the animal set, veterinarian Greg Tooke flies his Piper on countless house calls to far-flung ranches throughout eastern Montana and western South Dakota, often accompanied by a four-legged assistant, Peetie.

A few miles down the road from Littlefield is Post, population about 4,000, built from scratch in 1907 by C. W. Post, the cereal magnate. He wanted to establish a model, self-sufficient community, where farmers would grow cotton that town dwellers would weave and turn into finished products. Post believed that the roar of cannon would produce rainfall, and for several years before his death in 1914, he drove himself and the townspeople nearly crazy setting off explosions on the rimrock that surrounds Post. "He called them 'rain battles,' " writes Ed Syers in his guidebook, "and fought them from the cliff over the town, tying dynamite sticks to kites and bombarding any likely overcast." Results were mixed.

Today Post is quieter.

The local newspaper is the Post *Dispatch*. "The town was built on two-dollar oil," the city manager told me, "and spoiled by thirty-six-dollar oil. But we'll survive."

The Garza Theatre is on Main Street. Will McCrary, a veteran of 43 years of professional theater and movie experience in New York, California, and on the road, has helped his hometown put together a semi-professional band of performers. They stage eight shows a year, including, each July, something by Shakespeare. This year's was *Romeo and Juliet,* and I was there for the Saturday night performance.

The "star-crossed" teenagers, playing at love, "wedded to calamity," were as moving as always, and the death of Mercutio stirring and sad. Friar Lawrence was played by Will. "Ah, what an unkind hour / Is guilty of this lamentable chance!" he exclaimed, when he found Romeo dead in the tomb. As the theater cleared, I joined Will on stage and talked with him about his past and about drama in Garza.

"Back in 1985 I injured myself in a motorcycle accident and had to cancel some contracts. I hadn't seen my father for some time, so I came back to Post for a visit. Some people here asked me how to get a theater started, so I stayed around and helped them hold a couple of meetings, then another month to get them started on a show, then *another* month to get it on its feet. And I began to think, maybe this could turn into something interesting. The town fathers offered us this old movie theater, which had been boarded up for 30 years, but you could see the possibilities.

"I was disillusioned with the New York theater. The only things that're successful now are revivals or extravaganzas, and lawyers and bookkeepers are making many of the artistic decisions. So I stayed.

"The first years were tough, but we did quality productions and people

began to come. Now they come from all over West Texas. Lubbock, Amarillo. Vans will roll in with maybe 12 people. We try to do the best plays, the classic American plays from the last 20 or 30 years. Shakespeare's plays are hard, largely because they take such large casts. It was even harder with *The Tempest*—with all the little nymphs and sprites. There were armies of mothers downstairs trying to keep them quiet.

"Part of the heart of a community in the old days was the theater. People would meet together, laugh a little, cry a little, go away wiser. Once in a while an old cowboy will come in and say, 'My gosh, I can't believe y'all been doing this and I haven't been coming.' Live theater is not a part of their lives. Children love it. A little boy came in one day and said, 'The movie going to be again tonight?' I told him it was a play. He whispered to me, 'Two people die.' It's so real for them."

I told Will that I thought I had detected, during the balcony scene, a slight twang when Juliet said "Good night" to Romeo. He laughed. "You can't fight it. I try to stop people from saying 'git' and 'warsh.' We work on basic, horrible words, but there's a colorful edge to the drawl that makes it West Texas, and you can't erase it."

He sounded like a contented man. "This is where I'll . . . where I'll end up. This is it. I can never do any better than this. I didn't even know I was looking for this. It's like a gift that's come to me late in life."

Behind the wheel again: In Montana, the Big Sky Country, interstate exits are marked "Ranch Access," and abandoned houses on the homesteads are being used as corncribs. Hawks bob and sway in the sky like kites. The Fort Belknap Indian Reservation is golden in late summer. Towns along the High-Line—the Great Northern Railway—are shaped like T's: The grain elevators line the tracks, and Main Street is at a right angle to them. The elevators here are an indicator of a town's prosperity. Most of the wooden ones were built before 1942; if a town has only wooden elevators, it has slumped; towns with concrete elevators have been more prosperous. Southwest of Browning each vista is vaster than the last, and I think, this country can't get any bigger—and then it does. Driving east on Route 2, I see the Rocky Mountains in my rearview mirror.

The summer was nearing an end the day I found myself in Fort Benton for the Chouteau County Fair. Fort Benton was the upper limit of navigation on the Missouri for steamboats during the fur-trade era, and for miners headed for the goldfields of Idaho, Montana, and Canada. The arrival of the railroad killed the steamboat traffic, and the town has remained pretty quiet since then.

"Will Rudy the electrician please report to Carters Meat Balls," the PA system called as I arrived. A large oak tree sheltered the judging arena, an area of lush green grass with a few bleacher seats. A class of sheep was being judged as I sat down. A mother coached her daughter beside me. "He's really checking ears. Make sure your ears are clean." Old-timers in the bleachers were fussing about the savings and loan scandal. Then they discussed the deer alarms many people have installed in their cars to frighten deer off the highways. The question was whether they really work. "It depends on which way the deer is pointing when you scare it," said one.

Behind us on the Missouri River three snow geese took wing and headed upstream. The judges—not only for the sheep, but also for the cattle and the swine—were the same couple, Cathy and Shane Bessette, a mother-son team. I talked with them between events. "I started judging when I was in 4-H," said Cathy. "I went on to judging schools in Bozeman and Denver, and Shane followed along. Now we team-judge when we can. Our specialty is horses, but we do other things, too." I mentally contrasted the fair to the Iowa State Fair, which had employed 92 judges in 16 departments.

"The thing to remember about judging," said Shane, "is that, while you're judging the animals live, the important thing about them is how they'll hang in the cooler. These cattle will be sold at auction on Sunday and butchered Monday."

I dropped in on Cathy and Shane a few weeks later at their place—the K-Bar Stables—south of Great Falls. Here they board or train horses and offer lessons and practice facilities for ropers and riders who want to improve their rodeo skills. "When farming went bad a few years ago," Cathy told me, as we stood in the cool, dusty interior of the stables, "we sold out and bought this place. We weren't big enough to make it as farmers.

"In farming, we dealt with mother nature; here we deal with a different type of threat, you know? *Human* nature. Our family is able to handle this place pretty well. I've taught riding for 22 years and my daughter-in-law for 15. My daughter trains, and Shane's a licensed farrier."

We walked through the big stable. "We've got room for 60 head; there are 42 here now. Eight are ours, the others are boarding. We've got high hopes for this horse, Peewee, a jumper. He's already jumped four feet. And here's a famous horse, Snort. He jumped through a hotel window in the movie *El Diablo*. He made $28,000 last year and has his own money market account. So Shane's training one of ours to be a faller. This is Tawny. She's 22 years old and has had eight colts. Three years ago she came out of retirement, and she's winning again. I imagine she'll live to be 30 if we take good care of her." The sound of horses whinnying and blowing followed us through the stable. Two men were practicing roping steers in a dusty arena, with an excited dog running back and forth outside the fence. Frankly, it looked a little hard on the cattle. "I always say," said Shane's wife, Ardythe, "that all team ropers should come back as steers."

"The name Shane . . . ," I began. Cathy laughed. "I saw that movie ten times and cried every time. When that little boy follows Alan Ladd and calls, 'Shane! Come back!' I bawl every time." Wearing a leather apron and with a mouthful of nails, Shane had a horse's hind foot between his knees and was nailing on a new shoe. "Ho Bill," he murmured when I approached. I asked him how you get to be a licensed farrier. "I went to school for three months at Montana State University in Bozeman. Learned all about the bones in a horse's leg, how a horse should move, how to shoe him for whatever job he's doing. Then I passed the American Farriers Test, which means I'm licensed to shoe anywhere in the state."

Shane makes some of his own shoes and buys some in town. I told him I'd always thought it odd that horses needed shoes in the first place; surely it's a flaw in their design. "Really, any more, they're breeding little horses to have big feet, big horses to have little feet, they've kind of ruined the feet of horses." He took up a file and continued working on Bill's shoe. "In the old days—ho Bill—they seldom shod a horse. Like Indians. They didn't shoe their horses. Those were hard-footed horses, good-footed horses. If a horse went lame, they just turned him out. Gradually, he'd either get better or he wouldn't. I'm a firm believer that if a horse doesn't need shoes, don't shoe him." He straightened up and examined Bill's foot. "Well, it's on."

Few American Indians own horses today, but a number have maintained an interest in other animals. The Native American Fish & Wildlife

Society was incorporated in 1983 to help member tribes exchange information and management techniques dealing with the wildlife under their jurisdiction. In South Dakota I drove one morning to Eagle Butte, headquarters of the Cheyenne River Sioux Reservation, and found game warden Keith Annis, a member of the tribe, having an early morning cup of coffee. "Tribes and individuals can join the society," he told me. "Anyone, in fact, who's interested in the fish and wildlife resources of the American Indians. A need was felt for the society because the demand for fish and wildlife recreation has increased all over the country, and more pressure was being applied to tribal lands. American Indians have always been sensitive toward earth's resources, and we want to make sure that the environmental quality of our lives is not threatened."

Dennis Rousseau, Keith's boss, and Barry Betts, a biologist who does contract work for the tribe, joined us around a table in the fish and wildlife department's office. "It's ironic," said Barry. "American Indians were given land for their reservations that was terrible for farming—the ridges and the mountains and the badlands. All the worst land. But that land has turned out to be some of the richest in the country, in terms of its wildlife. The value of much of it a hundred years ago was zero; now it's priceless."

Keith, Dennis, and Barry loaded me into another van and off we went to

JOEL SARTORE

look at the reservation. The winter wheat was turning green, and prong-horns lifted their heads to stare as we drove by. American wigeons and god-wits on a shallow pond lifted off when a Northern harrier came over. Sharp-tailed grouse sat on fence posts, and small flocks of wild turkeys ambled through wooded stream bottoms. Fat prairie dogs made beelines for their holes. The countryside was desolate but beautiful.

"The reservation is open to hunting and fishing by non-Indians," Dennis told me. "They have to have our tribal license. Fishing season lasts all year. There are hunting seasons for deer, grouse, pheasants, partridge, coyotes, waterfowl. There's not a motel room to be had in this part of the state during pheasant season."

Lake Oahe, which is backed up behind the Oahe Dam at Pierre and is the reservation's eastern border, was down some 25 feet from the drought. "There's a big fight now with the Corps of Engineers," said Dennis. "They're taking water from us to keep barge traffic operating farther south."

Dennis told of visiting the Custer Battlefield National Monument and having to pay an entrance fee. He didn't think that was right. "Hey! We won!" That led to an exchange of Custer jokes. The best: Custer was heard to say, "I wonder what made them so mad; they were dancing last night."

The battlefield retains some of its eerie feeling, despite crowds of visitors. It's easy to visualize the lonely hilltop thick with encircling Indians and desperate troopers. I asked Doug McChristian, chief historian at the national monument, why, of all the battles fought during the Indian wars, this one was still so famous. "There are several reasons," he said. "For one, the country was in the midst of a national centennial celebration in Philadelphia and was beginning to consider itself quite an industrialized nation. Indian wars seemed like something from the distant past. And suddenly, quite unexpectedly, here was this great catastrophe: one of the most famous regiments in the army nearly wiped out and Custer himself killed. The 260 soldiers who died here represent nearly a third of all the battle casualties suffered by the army in a 30-year period. Also, a number of famous people came together here: Custer himself, a hero at the end of the Civil War, Sitting Bull, Gall, Crazy Horse. And there's the enduring mystery of what happened—something we'll probably never know.

"It was not only the army's greatest defeat, but also the Plains Indians' greatest victory. And, ironically, it lost them the war. People resolved to end the 'Indian problem' once and for all, and from there to the end it was relentless warfare. The Little Bighorn was not (Continued on page 156)

Trio of gunslingers blasts targets—some as small as quarters—tossed into the air near the ghost town of Kirkwell, Colorado. All three work with a tourist company that offers Old West trail and wagon rides and visits to rustic mining camps.

W*ild as ever the West was, a spirited mustang gallops across South Dakota plains, one of nearly 2,000 horses in a private sanctuary run by Dayton Hyde. Descended from conquistadores' mounts, feral mustangs transformed Plains Indian cultures. Many tribesmen turned from a life of farming to one of hunting bison on horseback. Today, swelling numbers of the horses threaten to overgraze private and public lands already committed to cattle. Annual mustang roundups reduce herd size and grazing pressures; some horses are adopted, others retire to sanctuaries.*

*T*all in the saddle at age seven, Cleve Fuller of Augusta, Montana, twirls a lariat before the admiring gaze of his father, Bruce. Riding and roping since he was two, Cleve shares the family's love of ranching. Often he practices with pet calf Michaelangelo (opposite), named for the Teenage Mutant Ninja Turtle; in trying to bulldog his calf to the ground, Cleve finds he has plenty of beef but not quite enough brawn. Today as in the past, plains children customarily take on adult tasks early, gaining experience and self-reliance.

only Custer's last stand, it was also the last stand of the American Indian."

Custer's star has ebbed and waned. Once he symbolized the conquering hero opening the American West to settlement; during the 1960s he came to represent for many everything brutal in the American character.

At times in the immense and abandoned plains, a surprising melancholy would settle upon me. A sadness would seem to drift up out of the lonely landscape, a sorrow to waft unexpectedly from the fields and hills. "The world is more beautiful than it is useful," wrote Thoreau. At such times, in search of diversion, I often looked for an auction. They're plentiful in the heartland these days. At one near Ponca City, Oklahoma, I could have acquired a Mickey Mouse telephone for three dollars.

Auctioneer: "Sold to the lady in the front row."

Auctioneer's assistant: "That's no lady. That's Mrs. Wilson."

An old-timer sidled up. "I remember threshing here years ago when there was just a little shack here. You could probably have bought it for $1,000 an acre then. Now they're hoping to get $7,500. It goes with the mineral rights. Can't ever tell. They'll put a well on 5 acres as quick as on 160." A black cat was having a good time threading through the crowd, but a tiny dog was confused and frightened.

Another day I wandered through the fairgrounds in Fargo, North Dakota, at an auction of seized farm equipment. Marshals had confiscated it in lieu of back taxes. A hundred or so men stood around talking, trying to keep

warm in the cold sun, chatting of yields and weather. Combines, trucks, harrows, plows, tractors, planters, big machines with folding wings—machinery I couldn't even identify. As I stood by an enormous corn planter, a man said, "Fill that up with corn and you could plant a section in a day."

"Half a section," said his son.

And in Battle Ground, Indiana, near the site of the battle of Tippecanoe, I stopped at an auction of household goods. The auctioneer was having trouble getting a bid on an old kerosene lantern. "What do you folks in Battle Ground do when the lights go out? None of my business, right?" In Missouri it was a long metal ladle that nobody seemed to want. The auctioneer held it up. "We used to have one of these on the farm. Used it to dip mice out of the cream before we hauled it to town to sell to the city slickers."

And finally, west of Bismarck, in a desolate section of emptiness, miles from anywhere, I came upon an auction of a forlorn ranch. Brown, rolling hills, bare of trees, bare of bushes—it looked the loneliest place on earth. Metal farm-implement toys—tractors and balers and corn planters—were by far the hottest items and were fetching practically as much as the real things. I bought a 12-volume *World's Popular Encyclopedia*, published in 1937, for a dollar. In it I read, of North Dakota, "surface consists mainly of plateaus, undulating plains, and grassy prairies; there are no trees. . . ."

The widow, a woebegone little old lady in a sweatshirt, was sitting on a bench watching her possessions being handled and bid for by strangers. I tried to talk with her. "How are you doing?" I asked.

"Not very well," she said, and looked away.

"How long did you live here?"

She turned to her daughter, and together they figured it out. "We moved here in 1934."

"You have a lot of memories, then, I guess."

"I guess so." She looked angry. She looked like she wished I'd go away.

"It was a ranch?" I asked.

"Grain and a few cattle," she said.

I was running out of conversation.

"Well, at least you had a nice day for your auction," I said.

She hugged her elbows. "It's chilly."

So I left her alone. An auction is fun only if it's not yours.

Rite of spring: Friends and hired hands work in teams in Nebraska's Sand Hills. They cut calves out from the herd one at a time for castration and branding.

FOLLOWING PAGES: Nudging cattle homeward, a Nebraska cowboy continues a seasonal tradition that has prevailed on the plains for more than 150 years.

And Tomorrow...

The Seeds of Change

Maybe we should put it back the way it was.

Maybe the heartland was too rich for its own good. To the pioneers, the land must have seemed indestructible, the resources inexhaustible, the limits unknowable. They believed that nothing they did could damage it, that no matter how they tried they could never use it up. So they were careless with the land, and it has paid a price, too.

In *Family Farming: A New Economic Vision,* Marty Strange writes, of American agronomy: "No system of agriculture brags more that it respects the soil, yet none has respected it less. We've done more damage to the topsoil of the Midwest in a hundred years of family farming than the communal cultures of the Native Americans did in a millennium. . . ." In the last 200 years, at least a third of our cropland topsoil has been lost.

The High Plains, or Ogallala, aquifer—one of the largest freshwater aquifers in the world—has been accumulating beneath the heartland for several million years. It underlies 174,050 square miles, and much of it is in trouble. In many irrigated areas of the plains, water is being pumped out of the Ogallala ten times faster than it is being restored.

Giant green circles visible from the air over the Great Plains mark the sites of center-pivot irrigators, each pumping up to 900 gallons of water a minute out of the aquifer. There are tens of thousands of them in the Great Plains. They water crops that are already subsidized and in surplus. Thus we mine fossil fuels in order to mine water and nutrients from the ground. The farm equipment, center-pivot irrigators, and trucks that haul food an average of 1,300 miles before someone eats it, all use energy. Nearly ten calories of energy are expended for every calorie of food grown and processed in the United States.

The political leaders and the U.S. Department of Agriculture seem helpless to come to grips with these issues. Journalist P. J. O'Rourke writes: "The USDA has 116,000 employees, about one for every three full-time

Prairie visionary and plant geneticist, Wes Jackson checks big bluestem at the Land Institute, a research center near Salina, Kansas. He advocates domesticating wild perennial species resistant to pests, drought, and disease. Such crops would not destroy topsoil or need fertilizers and pesticides.

PRECEDING PAGES: Harbingers of spring, pasqueflowers bring color to the still brown prairie. The blooms rotate on flexible stems to catch the sun.

farms in the country. These 116,000 people would be more useful to the farm economy if we sent them out to hoe weeds."

More than 50 percent of the nation's population now lives within 100 miles of a coastline, so the heartland is emptying. "Our schools train our children to leave," someone told me. Van Buren County, my home county, has 4,600 fewer people today than in 1850, four years after Iowa became a state. Some of the cities, too, are experiencing rough times. At eight o'clock on a Monday morning, I was literally the only customer in the airport at Topeka, capital of Kansas. And Oklahoma City was suffering through one of the oil industry's periodic slumps when I was there; an evening rush hour reminded me of Washington, D.C., on a Sunday afternoon.

In *Journal of a Prairie Year*, Paul Gruchow writes: "When the first white man arrived, there were as many elk and bison and antelope on the prairies as there are now cattle in all the United States. These creatures existed without benefit of tending, tractors, pesticides, barns, loans from the banks, without reference to the rise and fall of the world commodity markets, unmedicated, in a universe where nothing grew except a lot of, as we might say, weeds. Where there was not a straight row of anything to be seen from one horizon to the next horizon. It was a reasonably efficient arrangement."

There's nostalgia in the heartland so thick and rich you could cut it up and eat it like a pie. So maybe we should put the plains and prairies back the way they were.

The north and south forks of the Platte River rise in Colorado and join to flow through Nebraska. Once the river was broad and shallow, with numerous braids and sandbars. In spring, high water churned the sandbars and prevented vegetation from starting on them. In summer, when the sandbars were exposed, piping plovers and least terns built their nests on them. The water table was high, which kept adjacent meadows wet and full of migrating sandhill and whooping cranes. The central flyway of migratory birds through the continent is shaped like an hourglass, and its narrowest portion lies over the Platte River in central Nebraska. For millennia, hundreds of species of migrating birds have used the Platte and its meadows.

But after the Civil War, farmers in Wyoming and Colorado found that they could raise forage for cattle by capturing irrigation water from the Platte. "By 1901, summer flows of the Platte were overappropriated," John VanDerwalker told me. John is executive director of the Platte River Whooping Crane Maintenance Trust, Inc., in Grand Island, Nebraska. "There used to be three and a half million acre-feet of water flowing past Grand Island each year," he told me. "That's down to one million acre-feet. The sandbars have turned into wooded islands because they're no longer inundated by floods. Wooded islands are no use to migratory waterfowl. And a falling water table and riverside farming have dried up the meadows."

The trust is trying to restore an 80-mile stretch of the river, between Overton and Chapman—the so-called Big Bend area. In the late 1970s the Missouri Basin Power Project proposed a dam on the Laramie River in Wyoming. Nebraska and the National Wildlife Federation argued that it would seriously damage irrigated agriculture in western Nebraska and further degrade migratory bird habitat in the Big Bend area. Negotiation resulted in a settlement. In return for authorization to complete the dam, the power project funded the trust with a onetime payment of $7.5 million. Most of the interest from that money goes to buy riverside grasslands and croplands, which are restored for migratory bird use. Trust employees drive their machinery through the shallow water out to the islands, cut down trees and shred them, and disk the islands. Then they hope a flood will come to scour the islands and re-create the wide, braided river channels the birds prefer.

I drove with John through the Nebraska countryside alongside the Platte to see what kind of progress has been made. "If we, along with the Audubon Society, hadn't got to work," he told me, "all the safe tern and plover nesting habitat would have been eliminated by now, and the river would be nearly useless to cranes. Despite our efforts, almost 40 of the 80 miles of river have been abandoned by cranes in the last decade. This has resulted in a concentration of the crane population. In the areas we have rehabilitated, we now have 20,000 roosting cranes per mile of river. If a hail storm or tornado strikes, serious losses can occur." We drove along narrow gravel roads with slick, muddy spots on a cloudy day. Flocks of sandhill cranes with bright red caps stood in meadows and cornfields. As we passed, they turned their backs and walked away, looking over their shoulders at us. Their grating cries sounded like rusty machinery.

"Rivers cross the plains from west to east," said John. "They create a kind of ladder of habitats for migrating birds. The Platte is unique among these rivers because it flows across a wide, flat alluvial valley that historically had extensive wetlands. Water development and agriculture have had a devastating impact on Great Plains wildlife, and there seems to be no end to the destruction. Most of us don't recognize it because our perspective is limited. If we could live 300 years. . . .

"Imagine what you'd be thinking if you'd been alive in Jefferson's time and you could see what we've done to our country. You'd be alarmed."

Karen Cameron-Howell, wife of Kent Howell, in whose corn picker I had ridden in South Dakota, is district conservationist with the Soil Conservation Service in Brookings. She's been working on a major survey of water quality in South Dakota. "Urban people think we must have pretty good water out here. In fact the quality of our drinking water is poor. At our farm, Kent and I haven't drunk the water since probably 1982 or '83. I grew up in the Detroit suburbs, and I came out here thinking we'd have good water. But pesticides and nitrates have found their way into our groundwater."

I asked Karen if she and Kent qualified as one of the "small family farms" whose troubles we hear a lot about lately. *(Continued on page 176)*

*H*eadstones at Montana's Custer Battlefield National Monument mark the last stand of Lt. Col. George Armstrong Custer and his men against an encampment of Sioux and Cheyenne in 1876. Barbara A. Booher, of Northern Ute and Cherokee descent, became superintendent of the monument in 1989.

FOLLOWING PAGES: *Tracing the central flyway over the prairies, sandhill cranes pass above snow-dusted stubble in North Dakota on their fall migration south.*

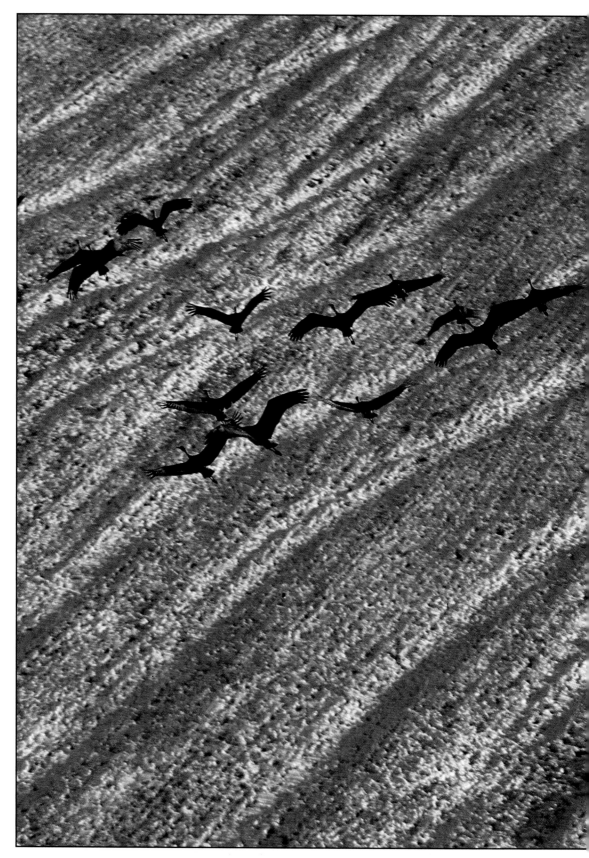

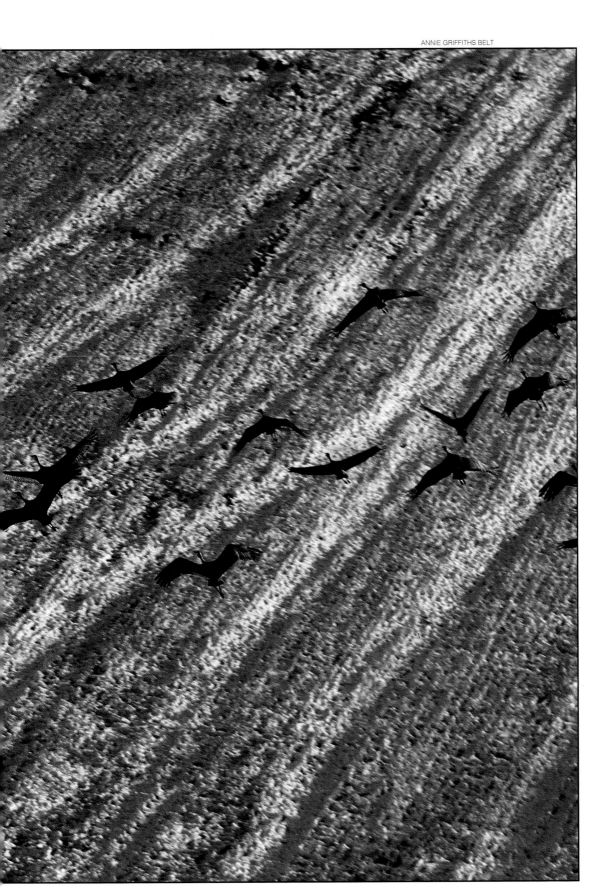

*B*lowing dust turns midday into twilight near Jamestown, North Dakota. Agriculture has stripped the cloak of grass from much prairie soil; the bare soil of the plowed land erodes easily in times of drought. At Konza Prairie (below), near Manhattan, Kansas, an embankment reveals the matted root systems that can grow down ten feet and bind the prairie soil.

FOLLOWING PAGES: *Controlled burning at Missouri's Prairie State Park rejuvenates the grass by removing the buildup of plant litter and recycling nutrients into the soil. Historically, fires kept woody plants from invading the prairies and stimulated grass growth.*

ANNIE GRIFFITHS BELT (BELOW); JOEL SARTORE (LEFT)

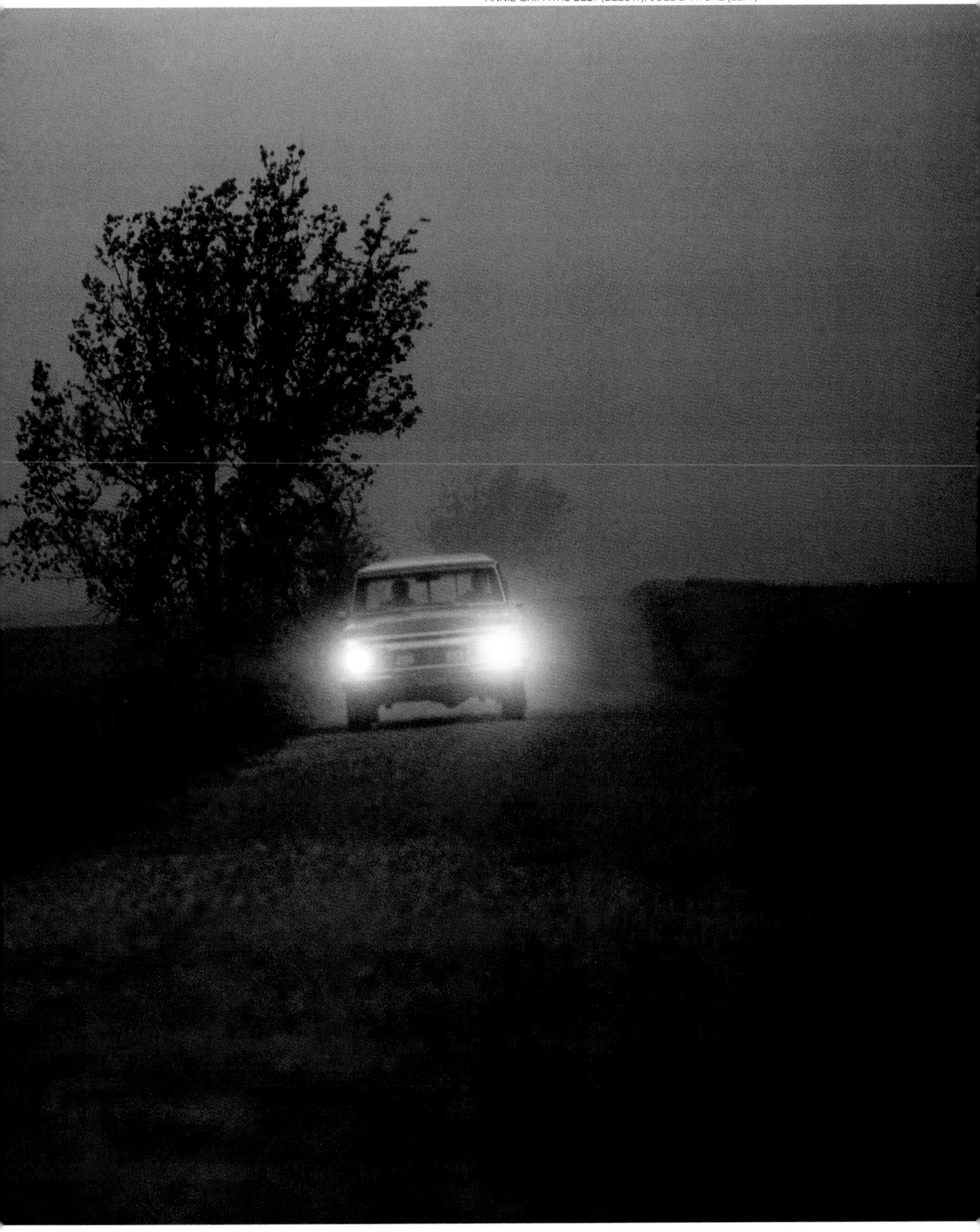

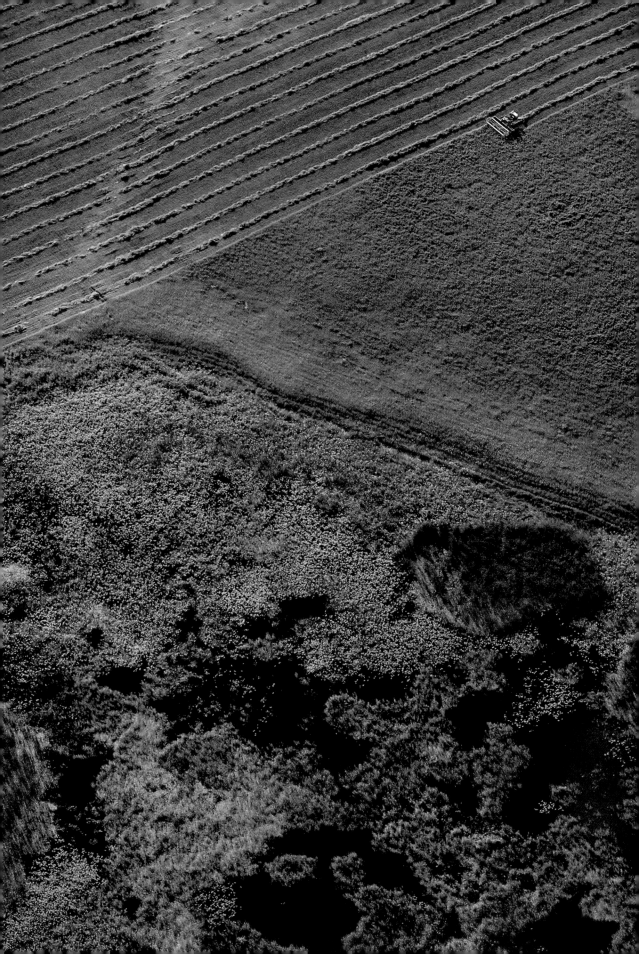

*M*ini-wilderness of marsh dappled with patches of open water survives
next to a partially cut field of alfalfa near Jamestown, North Dakota (opposite).
Pale areas in the wetland distinguish old stands from the light green of new-growth
cattails. Ice Age glaciers gouged thousands of shallow basins in the northern
grasslands. These prairie potholes fill with runoff from rain and snowmelt, forming
ponds and marshes. Famed as the "duck factory of North America," the prairie
pothole region serves as a nursery for about half of all wild ducklings bred on the
continent and sustains waterfowl and other migratory birds. But each year
farmers drain potholes for cropland. A grebe's nest (above) floats in a pothole in the
Samuel H. Ordway Memorial Prairie near Aberdeen, South Dakota. Water poses
no hazard to the chicks, which can swim a few hours after hatching.

"Size doesn't have much to do with how successful you are," she said. "Family farms still can make it *if* they manage their debt correctly, *if* they market their products properly, that kind of thing.

"There's another factor, one that makes me feel bad for some people: luck. Maybe you've made all the right decisions, but a catastrophe of some kind suddenly cuts your labor force in half, for instance. Or the bank, which has been sympathetic to you for years, suddenly gets pressure from its corporate owners to reduce its loan load by 5 percent. You're out of luck. I've heard of that happening several times."

People who love prairies often get together and talk about them, ramble through them, compare notes on them, and lament their passing. Of the 18 million acres of tallgrass prairie that Minnesota once had, less than one percent remains, and prairie-lovers cherish it. In mid-August, I journeyed north to Buffalo River State Park east of Moorhead for Prairie Day. A 2,000-acre remnant abuts the park. "There are 330 species of plants here in the Bluestem Prairie," Paul Rundell of the Minnesota Department of Natural Resources (DNR) told me, "and 30 weeks of season, from snow to snow, so things bloom every week." The Nature Conservancy owns Bluestem Prairie, and the Minnesota DNR helps manage it.

The 40 or 50 visitors sat on folding chairs in the fresh morning air for a program. A prairie manager talked about the difficulties of managing a prairie: "The jury's still out on whether we'll graze buffalo." Virgil Benoit, an associate professor of French at the University of North Dakota and a member of l'Association des Français du Nord, was costumed as Métis guide Pierre Bottineau. He told of a trip over the prairie in the winter of 1857: "The oxen's feet, cut by hard crustal snow, began to bleed, froze, and swelled to the size of hats." Peg Kohring, then executive director of the Minnesota chapter of the Nature Conservancy, talked about prairie flora and fauna, including prairie chickens: "If only human males could dance like that. . . ."

Later Peg, wearing a cool lavender hat, led a short prairie hike. "Plants don't want to be eaten," she told us, as we worked our way slowly through shin-high grasses and forbs. "They fight back with chemicals and smells." It was a hike that didn't cover much ground, for at every step or two Peg found another plant to talk about. "Lots of prairie plants are hairy to stop the wind from robbing moisture. This is prairie sage. It was used to worm dogs. Here's some goldenrod. There's a real war going on here. The goldenrod is trying to kill everything around it. This is called panic grass. Its smell was said to panic horses." Children frolicked around us, calling Peg's attention to other plants and fetching samples. "Chestnut-collared longspurs used to nest in the hoofprints of buffalo," she told them. "This is horsetail. It's called Indian tinkertoy, because you can take it apart." She brushed off her skirt. "We're all being pollinated."

The Minnesota chapter does not own a John Deere tractor, Peg told us then. It was John Deere's new steel plow that broke the prairie.

Nostalgic heartland people cling to their past. And to their conception of themselves. I tried to keep track of the organizations that use "heartland" in their names, but the list got too long. Kansas City evidently thinks of itself as the heart of the heartland, for the telephone book yielded more than 60 firms and organizations, from Heartland AIDS Resource Council to Heartland Yachts—not counting 40 listings for "Heart of America" entries. Lincolnites can patronize the Heartland Candy Company, and worshipers in Wichita can attend the Heartland Baptist Church. Topeka has a Heartland Park, and Des Moines a Heartland Inn. Oklahoma City has—or perhaps had—a Heartland Federal Savings & Loan.

Looking for lunch of regurgitated fish, an American white pelican nestling pokes its head into a parent's gullet at Chase Lake National Wildlife Refuge in North Dakota; the refuge shelters the largest colony of white pelicans in North America.

FOLLOWING PAGES: A great egret in the Crex Meadows Wildlife Area grips prey taken from a wetland formed in a glacial lake bed near Grantsburg, Wisconsin.

Changes are coming to the heartland. Some are small but may be connected to trends. The number of Amish in the United States—130,000—has doubled in the last 25 years, for instance, despite predictions that they would be assimilated. And some former heartlanders are returning. Barry Betts and his wife, Janine, both natives of South Dakota, lived for a time in Manassas, Virginia, and commuted to Washington, D.C. Tired of the urban life, they sat down one day to choose a new place to live. "We each made a list of the places we'd like to move to," Barry told me. "And at the top of both lists was South Dakota."

Some areas are adapting to the changes. Several small heartland cities have attracted telecommunications firms. Chances are, if you call a catalog's toll-free number, you'll speak with an operator in the heartland. The operators are courteous and well educated, they have neutral accents, and, being equidistant from both coasts, represent a compromise with the time zones.

The Midwestern boosterism that Sinclair Lewis wrote of has changed; towns still shout of their excellence, but today their goal is not simply economic growth, but survival. In Iowa, Van Buren County's hamlets have joined forces to promote themselves as the Villages of Van Buren. On various weekends of the year, one will host a strawberry festival, one the Fourth of July celebration, another a flea market. In August, Bike Van Buren floods the county with riders, and during a weekend in October a Scenic Drive and Forest Craft Festival takes place county-wide. Weavers and potters will set up in one village; woodworkers will demonstrate in a local state park.

An intriguing change in the heartland involves Native Americans, whose numbers are suddenly increasing far faster than can be accounted for by a high birthrate or improved medical care. Bob Ferguson, historian for the Mississippi band of the Choctaw Indians, says, "For many decades, it wasn't fashionable to be Indian. If you had Indian ancestry, you didn't admit it. Now, it's all-American." According to the 1990 census, the number has increased from 523,600 in 1960 to 1.9 million.

At Custer Battlefield National Monument in Montana the new superintendent is Barbara A. Booher, of Cherokee and Northern Ute descent. An Indian woman in charge of the Custer battlefield! The Custer buffs, of whom there are many, are not all pleased. "They must feel they're losing the Battle of the Little Bighorn all over again," I said to Barbara. "They probably do. I haven't asked them," she replied.

I found her cool and calm and clearly in charge in her office at the monument. I asked her if she had studied Custer in school on the reservation. "Yes," she said, "we studied Custer. When I attended school, U.S. history emphasized the military's accomplishments. If Indians were even mentioned, it was in a negative sense. 'The only good Indian is a dead Indian,' is what my eighth-grade teacher taught us.

"Most people who come here go first to Last Stand Hill, where they naturally identify with the army—making its last stand. They should visit the valley—where the Indian encampment was. The valley was the site of the initial attack on the Indians."

Barbara was quoted by the *Denver Post* as saying, "This is the only battlefield where all the monuments are to the losers"—which also failed to endear her to the Custer buffs. Soon after I left, she journeyed to Washington to participate in a congressional hearing. The National Park Service was testifying in favor of a monument to the American Indians who fought at the Little Bighorn. Said Congressman John J. Rhodes III, Republican of Arizona, "This legislation is to honor the Cheyenne, Sioux, and other Indian nations who gave their lives to defend their families, life-style, culture and their lands." At last report the bill had passed the House of Representatives.

Of America's plains and prairies, the future looks darkest for the plains, long considered "flyover" country by many, an area to be leaped across to get to California. The rivers of the plains flow eastward, a pattern for the railroads and the interstate highways. Several interstates run from east to west across the Great Plains, but only one—I-25—crosses it from north to south, and it hugs the Rocky Mountains.

Many believe that pushing agriculture beyond the 100th meridian—or the line of 20 inches of rainfall—by offering settlers cheap homesteads was a mistake we have been paying for ever since. With their economies propped up by the federal government—through huge military bases, through price support payments for corn and wheat, through subsidized water for irrigation and subsidized grass for grazing—the plains states may see some changes in their futures.

A husband-and-wife team from Rutgers University in New Jersey—Frank and Deborah Popper—have been looking at the Great Plains and making predictions and proposals based on what they are seeing. They think much of the Great Plains ought to be given back to the buffalo and the Indians. The Poppers analyzed the plains states county by county, identifying those they call "distressed"—counties with 4 people per square mile or fewer, counties that have lost at least 50 percent of their population since 1930, counties that lost at least 10 percent of their population between 1980 and 1988, counties with a median population age 35 or higher, counties with 20 percent or more of their people living in poverty, counties that spend $50 or less per capita per year on new construction. Such distressed counties make up about a fourth of the Great Plains, cover 139,000 square miles, and contain 413,000 people, almost the same number that live in Oklahoma City. As depopulation continues—and it does: Between 1980 and 1990, North Dakota lost 13,917 people, more than 2 percent of its 1980 population of 652,717—the Poppers think the government should begin buying up land from willing sellers, tearing down the fences, planting native grasses to hold the soil, and reintroducing bison and other wildlife, creating, in fact, the "Buffalo Commons." *(Continued on page 186)*

"We wanted to keep this pretty place the way it is for forever and a day," says farmer Ernest Lundblad, holding a summer bouquet in Minnesota's Lundblad Prairie. In a state where 99 percent of the native prairie has vanished, his family kept 80 acres from the plow. The Nature Conservancy, a private nonprofit group that manages 168 prairie reserves, bought the tract in 1983. The Conservancy also owns 284-acre Clymer Meadow, near Celeste, Texas, where Lois Lewis, 92, roamed the grasslands as a girl.

Ablaze with bright spires of gayfeather, a restored prairie at the University of Wisconsin Arboretum in Madison evokes the splendor of the unplowed grasslands (opposite). Wildflowers planted half a century ago on an abandoned farm, now named Curtis Prairie, produce a succession of bright blooms from early spring until November. On average, a dozen species come into flower each week. Black-eyed Susans and tall, gray-headed coneflowers (above) accent another expanse of the Curtis Prairie. The Curtis, reclaimed in the 1930s, demonstrates that some prairies can be restored successfully. Spiderwort seeds collected in a field of big bluestem will be used to reestablish more prairie.

"It is difficult to predict the future course of the plains' ordeal," they have said. "The most likely possibility is a continuation of trends that go back to the twenties: a long-term, painful draining. . . . The most intriguing alternative would be to restore large parts of the plains to its pre-settlement condition, to make it again the commons the settlers found in the 19th century. This approach would for the first time recognize its unsuitability for agriculture."

When I heard that the Poppers were speaking at the 1990 Prairie Festival at the Land Institute, near Salina, Kansas, I made it a point to attend.

Wes and Dana Jackson co-founded the Land Institute in 1976 as "a non-profit educational-research organization devoted to sustainable agriculture and good stewardship of the earth." The Jacksons and a staff of 12 operate the institute now. The theme of the 1990 festival was "The Future of Prairie Communities."

I found several hundred interested people attending workshops on the Future of Plains Agriculture, on Native American Communities, on Current Topics in Farm Politics, on Rural Communities and Their Schools. They were an intense and serious crowd, deeply concerned with the issues they had come to explore, and the buildings and grounds of the Land Institute echoed with their arguments.

The Poppers made their presentation—The Fate of the Plains—on Saturday afternoon to a standing-room-only crowd. Maps highlighted the distressed counties. "Although the plains cover a fifth of the landmass of the lower 48 states," said Deborah, "they contain less than 3 percent of the country's population—and they're losing that. Fifty of Nebraska's 93 counties have 50 percent fewer people in them now than in 1930."

Frank spoke, too. "We tried to force waterless, treeless steppes to behave like Ohio," he said.

"No state is entirely within the Great Plains," they pointed out, "but ten are partially. The plains have suffered through two major boom-and-bust cycles—those culminating in the 1890s and the 1930s—and the one that's occurring now may finish the job of depopulating much of the region. People are voting with their feet.

"These are the unhappy factors confronting the plains: Soil erosion is up; a serious shortage of water looms; we're heading into another economic downturn; the drought is hanging on; Americans' dietary habits are turning them away from beef; the savings and loan crisis hit the plains hard; even foreign affairs are affecting the plains adversely—as tension lessens between the U.S. and the U.S.S.R., military bases will be closed.

"Today, in some areas of the Great Plains, 60 percent of the income is federal: from Social Security, crop subsidies and agricultural programs, and federal payrolls."

It was a sobering presentation, and we stood in somber clumps afterward to talk about it. For it makes an intriguing picture—the Great Plains again the domain of bison and coyotes and prairie dogs.

It makes the problems of the prairie states seem more manageable. But even there, it's becoming apparent that changes must be made in the way agriculture is practiced. Huge, flat fields plowed and planted in straight furrows make a farmer's use of his machinery efficient, but they lead to wind erosion, and furrows that run up and down hills send tons of topsoil streaming toward the ocean. Fly across the prairie today and the wonder is that any soil is left at all, so turbid and brown are the streams and rivers. Chemicals can control pests and weeds, but at the cost of water quality. Of 686 rural wells tested in Iowa, nearly 15 percent are contaminated with one or more pesticides.

Perhaps one of the country's most thoughtful spokesmen for sustainable agriculture is Wes Jackson, and when the turmoil of the prairie festival had subsided and life was back to normal, I joined him and Dana for a meal

To give people a better understanding of the grasslands, arboretum employee Brock Woods conducts a tour at the University of Wisconsin's Curtis Prairie. "We want people to come out to see, touch, and smell the rich variety of sights, textures, and aromas," says Woods, showing visitors a leafhopper in a bug box.

ANNIE GRIFFITHS BELT

at a Chinese restaurant in Salina. I asked them what mistakes had been made in our dealing with the land in the heartland.

"Plowing west of the 100th meridian should have been greatly limited," said Wes. "That's right at the point where evaporation exceeds rainfall. And agriculture is destructive to the land when you move it to the hillsides. We should have stayed in the valleys. We could have raised wheat on flat, non-eroding ground and had plenty. Too, we should have stuck to buffalo instead of switching over to cattle. For one thing, you don't have to worry about them in the wintertime."

For another, bison is high in protein but lower in fat, cholesterol, and calories than most other meats, including poultry and some kinds of fish.

"Homesteading—that was a mistake," said Wes. "It was a result of Jefferson's fascination with geometry, with the grid, with the idea of imposing order on a nonrational world."

Dana said, "John Wesley Powell argued that land in the West needed to be distributed according to the available water, not on the basis of 160 acres for everyone."

"He argued that point to Congress," said Wes. "Boy, if you read those accounts! Congressmen were as stupid then as they are now. The idea that rain would follow the plow! People get carried away with their own eloquence."

He poured more tea.

"It was a mistake to introduce new grasses. There was not a thing wrong with the vegetative structure we had. Now, if you drive the interstates in this country, it's a bromegrass world all the way to Canada." Bromegrass is a weedy invader from Europe.

Wes's fortune cookie read, "You look for the best in each situation and person that you encounter."

The Land Institute accepts as many as ten interns each year. Along with staff scientists, they do research in a number of experimental plots, trying to develop or breed perennial grain crops—crops that would reproduce themselves each year, thus eliminating the need for plowing. When you plow the prairie, water escapes in evaporation, and if it rains, soil rushes toward the nearest river. To a sustainable agriculture person, the plow is the devil. One experiment of the institute attempts to convert grain sorghum to a winter-hardy perennial by crossing it with a weedy relative. Another is trying to domesticate Illinois bundleflower—an herbaceous legume—as a perennial grain crop.

After our Chinese meal, we drove out to the institute, and as the summer evening gathered itself toward nightfall, Wes and I walked for a while across the prairie. Grasses swished at our ankles, and crickets chirped. A few mosquitoes came buzzing around. We munched juicy plums from a tree near the house. "We've been eating these for a week," Wes said. "There are still too many to keep up with. If you want to go the organic trip, pears, cherries, plums—those are the things. Peaches are no good here, apricots no good. You should spray apples. But we're such ecological Baptists around here. . . ." As we walked, we talked. On Christianity: "We may have begun abusing our land when we switched from the pantheism of the Indians to the monotheism of Christianity," Wes said. "To the Indians, everything had a soul or a spirit—the land, the rocks, the water. When you used those things, you did it with reverence."

A neighbor's small herd of buffalo moseyed across a hillside.

Like tombstones, an abandoned car and a lonely church near Gilead, Nebraska, mark the end of the era, before population and income declined on the Great Plains.

FOLLOWING PAGES: An empty farmhouse near Fargo, North Dakota, speaks of the hard times that have driven heartland farmers out of business. Recurring droughts and low crop prices in a glutted market have plunged many into debt.

On prairies: "See the other side of the fence? That's native prairie that's never been plowed. This side, we've revegetated. We can come close to reproducing the general aspect of historic prairies, but we can't give them the diversity they had. . . . Here's some eastern gama grass, relative of corn. It's 27 percent protein, three times that of corn, twice that of wheat. This is one of our stars. . . . Here's some of our sorghum, which we're crossing with Johnson grass, a perennial, trying to get a winter-hardy sorghum. Prairies evolved to absorb and hold as much water as possible, whereas wheat and corn tend to give it up. Rootedness is what protects."

We stepped over a low fence. "This is native prairie that was a wheat field. We planted it back five or six years ago. That's ecological restoration. I think it looks pretty good." And another fence. "Now this has never been plowed. We're in what Zebulon Pike saw. You can see why they compared it to the ocean. Also why they said it was like plowing through a heavy woven doormat. They say it sounded like the opening of a zipper. Imagine what that was like. If you squat down, so you can't see the houses, there's an illusion of a former reality." We did. "Here's some gayfeather. That'll have a beautiful purple flower."

On human nature: "Power refuses to acknowledge ignorance. I start with the assumption that humans are going to be stupid and wicked."

"But don't your interns make you hopeful about the future of agriculture?" I asked. "They're idealistic and smart, but we've had idealism and intelligence for a long time. And in a way, it's irrelevant how they make me feel. I'd be doing this anyway."

The sun dropped nearer the horizon, and the mellow golden light seemed to come up out of the ground. Walt Whitman described a prairie sunset: "Shot gold, maroon and violet, dazzling silver, emerald, fawn, / . . . colors till now unknown. . . ."

"Here's some lead plant. Isn't that pretty? We could have had the lead plant for its beauty, and we could have had the buffalo for meat. Down in the valleys we could have grown our corn and our wheat."

We stood and watched the bison as the light failed. "There's a quote by biochemist George Wald that I like." He recited from memory this passage by the 1967 Nobel laureate: "We living things are the late outgrowth of the metabolism of our galaxy. Carbon, which was entered so importantly in our bodies, was cooked in the remote past of a dying star. From it, at lower temperatures, came nitrogen and oxygen. These our indispensable elements were spewed out into space, to mix, to form planets, and eventually us, ourselves. The ancient seas set the pattern of ions in our blood; the ancient atmospheres molded our metabolism. . . ."

Children of a dying star, Wes calls us, and compares us to Odysseus in the sacred dwelling of Circe, sated with pleasure and reluctant to come out to face our destinies. He tells of an old-timer, a native Kansan born in 1908, whose father once took him to a nearby canyon. There a band of Indians had pushed a threshing machine over a cliff. Trying to put things back the way they were.

I miss the heartland, its courtesy and warmth and reserve, its plains and prairies, its sunsets and moonrises. Heartland is two words, heart and land, and that's how I think of it: the heart of my land. I think too of Abigail Malick, whose son Hiram drowned in the Platte River in 1848. For the next 17 years, she wrote to the family members she had left behind, far away on the other side of the enormous and windswept heartland. "My o dere children. I wish that you were heare."

She paid a price.

Advocate of a Flint Hills Prairie National Monument, National Audubon Society representative Ron Klataske closes a gate at the 10,894-acre Z-Bar Ranch, near Strong City, Kansas. The Audubon Society proposes the property as the first national tallgrass prairie preserve. Grazed but never plowed, it could be restored to let Americans experience the almost forgotten spectacle of the prairie landscape.

FOLLOWING PAGES: Sunrise shadows and early mist mute the beauty of the Flint Hills.

Notes on Contributors

The author and principal photographers bring to this book pride in their heartland heritage.

Author RON FISHER lived first on a farm, then in a village in Iowa. While attending the University of Iowa, he spent summers working for small newspapers. Ron joined the National Geographic staff in 1962.

ANNIE GRIFFITHS BELT, born and reared in Minneapolis, worked for Minnesota newspapers. Her photographs have appeared in many NATIONAL GEOGRAPHIC magazine articles and in several of the Society's books.

Kansas born and educated, GEORGE OLSON gained photographic experience on Kansas newspapers. His National Geographic assignments began in 1977 and include the Special Publication *Nature on the Rampage*.

JOEL SARTORE was born in Oklahoma and grew up in Nebraska. He became director of photography at the *Wichita Eagle*. Joel launched his free-lance career in 1991 with a NATIONAL GEOGRAPHIC magazine assignment.

Additional Reading

Readers may consult the *National Geographic Index* for related articles and books. Of particular interest is "The Tallgrass Prairie: Can It Be Saved?" by Dennis Farney in the January 1980 NATIONAL GEOGRAPHIC. The following books may prove helpful: E. C. "Teddy Blue" Abbot, *We Pointed Them North*; Claude A. Barr, *Jewels of the Plains: Wildflowers of the Great Plains Grasslands and Hills*; Warren A. Beck and Ynez D. Haase, *Historical Atlas of the American West*; Lauren Brown, *Audubon Society Nature Guides: Grasslands*; Tom C. Cooper, ed., *Iowa's Natural Heritage*; David F. Costello, *The Prairie World*; Patricia D. Duncan, *Tallgrass Prairie: The Inland Sea*; Ian Frazier, *Great Plains*; Georg Gerster, *Amber Waves of Grain: America's Farmlands from Above*; Paul Gruchow, *Journal of a Prairie Year*; Wes Jackson, *New Roots for Agriculture*; James H. Madison, ed., *Heartland: Comparative Histories of the Midwestern States*; John Madson, *Where the Sky Began: Land of the Tallgrass Prairie*; Mil Penner and Carol Schmidt, *Prairie: The Land and Its People*; O. J. Reichman, *Konza Prairie: A Tallgrass Natural History*; John Running, *Honor Dance: Native American Photographs*; Lillian Schlissel, Byrd Gibbens, and Elizabeth Hampsten, *Far From Home: Families of the Westward Journey*; George R. Stewart, *Names on the Land*; Marty Strange, *Family Farming: A New Economic Vision*; Bob Waldon, *A Prairie Guide to Feeding Winter Birds*; Walter Prescott Webb, *The Great Plains*; Suzanne Winckler, *The Smithsonian Guide to Historic America: The Plains States*.

JOEL SARTORE

DOROTHY DAVIS, 1990 BEAUTY QUEEN, GREETS KANSANS.

Acknowledgments

The Book Division wishes to thank the organizations and other individuals named or quoted in the text, and those cited here: JoAnn Arms, Denise Barker, Kathryn Belcher, Lou Bennett, Shirlyn Bentley, Rebecca Bernard, Kirk L. Bjornsgaard, Ronald L. Bode, David S. Boyd, Roger A. Bruns, Adrianne B. Burk, Ruth Chama, Kim Alan Chapman, Captain Cook, Donald Dean Coolidge, Lou Cowardin, Robert Dierkes, Russ Drafahl, Jack T. Dugan, Gale Dunkhas, Miriam Dunlap, Barbara Penfold Ferry, Jon P. Finney, Mary Ford, Red Fourkiller, Judith A. Franke, Bruce and Nancy Fuller, Beth Gibans, Mike Haberkorn, Eldon Harding, Jeffrey O. Heeb, John A. Hostetler, Lynn Howard, Myles Johnson, Phyllis Johnson, John Karras, James E. Kennel, Paul A. Kooiker, Lorence Larson, Karl Ledbetter, Dixie Legler, Marian Malek, Victor Martin, Mason May, James R. McLaughlin, Connie Menninger, Gary Smith Merrill, Ben Moffett, Jake Moore, Robert L. Moore, Jr., Daniel G. Morrical, Mary Muir, Carol Nachtigall, Louise A. Nettleton, Linda Okeson, John L. O'Neill, Jim Owens, Richard F. Palazzo, Jon Piper, William B. Preston, Cynthia Rahjes, Mark Reinhard, Daryl Richter, Robert C. Ripley, Kiki Rosatti, Duffy Sauer, Matt A. Scherer III, Reuben H. Schleifer, A. H. Schollett, Mary Sederburg, Gregory E. Siekaniec, Cleo Seimers, Tom Simons, Peggy Smith, Kathy Stender, Kathie Swift, Jake Vail, Walt Vernon, William D. Welge, Buck Westbrook, Geraldine Wortas, Benedict K. Zobrist. We are especially grateful for the assistance of Arnold Leaderbrand and Will McCrary, who died during the production of this Special Publication.

The Malik family papers (pages 10 and 193) are housed in the Beinecke Rare Books and Manuscript Library, Yale University Library, New Haven, Connecticut. Information for vegetation zones shown on the map (page 6) is based on *The Prairie World* by David F. Costello, p. 39.

Index

Library of Congress CIP Data
Fisher, Ronald M.
Heartland of a continent : America's plains and prairies / by Ron Fisher.
p. cm.
Includes index.
ISBN 0-87044-830-7
1. West (U.S.)--Geography.   2. Middle West--Geography.   3. Great Plains--
Geography.   4. Prairie Provinces--Geography.   5. Plains—North America.
6. Prairies--North America.   I. National Geographic Society (U.S.)   II. Title.
F595.3.F57 1991
978'.03--dc20   91-33546
                                                                                                      CIP

Composition for this book by the Typographic section of National Geographic Produc-
tion Services, Pre-Press Division. Set in Palatino. Printed and bound by R. R. Donnel-
ley & Sons, Willard, Ohio. Color separations by Graphic Art Service, Inc., Nashville,
Tenn.; Lanman Progressive Co., Washington, D. C.; Lincoln Graphics, Inc., Cherry
Hill, N.J.; NEC, Inc., Nashville, Tenn.; and Phototype Color Graphics, Pennsauken,
N.J. Dust jacket printed by Federated Lithographers-Printers, Inc., Providence, R.I.

NATIONAL GEOGRAPHIC MAGAZINE

GILBERT M. GROSVENOR, *President and Chairman*
WILLIAM GRAVES, *Editor*